Praise from professional money managers:

"Hide this book in a safe place because grossly overpaid investment advisors are burning every copy they can find."

—Rick Ferri, CFA, President, Portfolio Solutions LLC
Author: *All About Asset Allocation,*
All About Index Funds, and others.

"Rick has produced a masterful financial guide for beginning investors and old hands alike. If you want to get started investing the right way, this book provides the clarity *and* backbone to achieve your financial destiny."

—Bill Schultheis, Financial Adviser
Author: *The New Coffeehouse Investor*

"Rick has provided a great service. In terms that the novice investor can understand, he provides ten simple rules that provide the prescription for investment success. In fact, if you follow his rules you are virtually guaranteed to outperform the majority of investors, both individual and professionals alike."

—Larry Swedroe, Principal and Director of Research
Buckingham Family of Financial Services
Author of eleven books on investing

"Crisp, simple, and irrefutably great investment advice."

—Allan S. Roth, CBS MoneyWatch columnist
Author: *Dare To Be Dull*

D1572688

Praise from academics:

"Here are 10 simple, easy to follow, and proven investing rules. Investing an hour reading this short book will make you a better investor."

—Burton G. Malkiel, Princeton University, Professor of Economics
Author: *A Random Walk Down Wall Street*

Praise from other respected authors:

"*Common Sense Investing* captures the core elements of the Bogleheads® investment philosophy in terms any investor can easily understand and implement. Read it and reap!"

—Mel Lindauer, Forbes columnist,
Co-author: *The Bogleheads' Guide to Investing*
and *The Bogleheads' Guide to Retirement Planning*

"Rick makes it super-simple to understand personal finance, regardless of your skill level. This book, along with his creative and straight-forward streaming videos, will get you and your money heading in the right direction."

—Jeff Lehman
Author: *The Frugal Millionaires*
and *First Job~First Paycheck*

"Rick has a gift for distilling the essence of a topic, and presenting it in a way that produces an *Oh, I Get It!* insight."

—Chris Smith
Author: *Securing Your Financial Future*

Praise for the associated free online videos:

"Awesome videos of common sense investing/finances, with top shelf production values."

—Jeff MC
Bogleheads forum comment

"These are perfect, well organized explanations."

—Boglenaut
Bogleheads forum comment

"I enjoy the casual wear, calm, low-key approach to these serious and often complex subjects (especially liked the chef's outfit)."

—Fallible
Bogleheads forum comment

"Bogleheads never cease to amaze me with the effort put forth to help others improve their own financial lives."

—Staythecourse
Bogleheads forum comment

"Those videos are fantastic!"

—Raging Mage
Bogleheads forum comment

"Absolutely terrific. I can think of several friends who NEED to watch these."

—Shariron
Bogleheads forum comment

"Fantastic information and great presentation! Thanks so much. I'm sharing this link with my friends and family."

—Mike J.
comment left on FinancingLife.org website

"Thanks! I am new to investing and these videos help me understand very easily."

—William
comment left on FinancingLife.org website

"Thank you for using your considerable gifts to help people. And God bless Jack Bogle!"

—Martha
comment left on FinancingLife.org website

COMMON SENSE INVESTING

Also by Rick Van Ness

Why Bother With Bonds

A Guide To Build All-Weather Portfolio Including CDs,
Bonds, and Bond Funds—Even During Low Interest Rates

COMMON SENSE INVESTING

Ten Simple Rules to Finance Your Dreams

or

Create a Roadmap to

Achieve Financial Independence

Rick Van Ness

Edited by Jennifer Howell

Published by GrowthConnection, LLC
Mukilteo, Washington, USA

Author Online

Find explanatory videos, smart tips,
and links to useful resources at
www.FinancingLife.org
rick@financinglife.org

Published by GrowthConnection, LLC

Use of Proceeds

100% of the revenue from sales of this book will be applied towards promoting financial literacy through bite-sized videos, short books, the Bogleheads' wiki, and other educational projects.

Comments and feedback welcomed and appreciated!

The author welcomes and appreciates all thoughts and suggestions. Reach him at: rick@financinglife.org

ISBN: 978-0985800413 (Paperback)

Library of Congress Control Number: 2011937158

Printed in the United States of America.
Version 2.0

Dedication

To John C. Bogle, champion of ordinary investors, who points out the common sense amid all the noise and confusion. You helped me see the difference between investing and speculating, and the genius in common sense.

~ ~ ~

To all Bogleheads. I learn from each of you. And more than anything, you've all been role models—generously sharing your wisdom, often anonymously.

~ ~ ~

To each of you readers who have selected this book because your dreams will need money. May all your dreams come true!

Table of Contents

Personal finance is a means to an end—living a rich and fulfilling life. It is not hard. It is not complicated. I write this to share simple truths I've learned from some very wise people.

—Rick Van Ness

Preface (a true story)

Years ago, our company had occasional luncheon speakers. I clearly remember the poster advertising one of these. It had the name of Vicki Robin's book, but all I saw was *Bla bla bla bla bla bla Achieving Financial Independence*. I snuffed with the arrogance of an MBA from a top university on Wall Street (ink still wet): *"What could they teach me about finances!"* Instead, I worked during this lunchtime presentation at my desk and went down to grab a quick bite afterwards. The cafeteria was empty. I sat alone.

After their event, the host brought the speakers in and joined me for lunch. I said hello but mostly listened. My ears were burning. I couldn't believe what I was hearing. *"Excuse me?"* I asked one of the two presenters. I then learned that she had worked for a dozen years, saving most of what she earned, and was now living entirely off the investment dividends. *"How could you do that?"* They were making different kind of choices than most of us: clothing from thrift stores (I couldn't tell), bartering for car repairs, etc. But they woke up every morning free to spend their time exactly as they chose! They volunteered for causes that were important to them. This was powerful! While I had thought their talk was about *finances*, it was really about *achieving independence*!

They hadn't published their book *Your Money or Your Life* yet, but it was available on audio cassettes and they left a copy for our company library. I borrowed my young son's bright red cassette player and listened to six cassettes on a flight to Chicago, and the remaining six on my flight home. They spoke about fulfillment in a personal and non-judgmental way, fully recognizing that it varies from one individual to the next. They spoke about "going to work" as trading "life energy" for money, which is both enlightening and extremely helpful for making purchase decisions: *"How much life energy would I really want to trade for that Stuff?"* They put into words what I knew to be true.

Ever since, I have been keenly aware and proudly frugal. I have also learned quite a bit more about common sense investing. Now, I too wake up every morning with the *freedom* to spend my time as I choose. I hope my books and videos help you to achieve the same, and to make the most of our precious lives.

The beginning is the most important part of the work.

—Plato, *The Republic*

Introduction

If you are like most of us, you are busy living your life and just not interested in becoming an expert in investing. My goal is to show you that it's actually not hard to take control of your finances, save and invest wisely, and then get on with your life with a sound financial lifestyle that will support your dreams. You are going to learn how to correctly buy and hold a diversified portfolio of stocks and bonds for the long term.

Start by tuning out all the shows and newsletters trying to sell you something. For us, there is no better mentor than legendary mutual fund industry veteran John C. Bogle. We'll also incorporate the work of a few Nobel Laureates and distinguished academics. Quite frankly, it is the advice I wish I heard when I was 25 years old. We'll develop four general principles as 10 simple rules.

Start saving now, not later

The first two rules are all about getting started, and finding a way to save a portion of what you earn. If you can't do this, the other eight rules are moot. There are some great tips in here, so I hope you'll find these helpful.

- Rule #1: Develop a workable plan

- Rule #2: Invest early and often

Diversify your investments

If starting to save now is the most important habit you need to form, the way that you then allocate this to stocks and bonds is the most important decision you need to make. *Diversify your investments.* I know you think you know what this means, but most people actually don't. These will be our next three rules. It's not hard, but since this is all about risk management and it is *so* important, read up and make sure you grasp these simple concepts.

- Rule #3: Never bear too much or too little risk

- Rule #4: Diversify!

- Rule #5: Never try to time the market

Minimize costs

Small percentages make a *huge* difference over the course of our lifetime. Our next three rules will show you how you can keep what you earn by not giving it away in unnecessary fees and taxes.

- Rule #6: Use index funds when possible

- Rule #7: Keep costs low

- Rule #8: Minimize taxes

Stick to your Plan!

Our last rules will help you create a simple one-page written plan— and that very action will help give you the discipline to stick with these time proven rules that we'll now explore individually in more detail.

- Rule #9: Keep it simple

- Rule #10: Stay the course

Each of these rules are a short chapter. You can read them from start to finish or skip ahead to any of particular interest.

Each of these rules is also a short explanatory video that may be viewed for free in high-definition streaming video at www.financinglife.org. This book complements the video series to read offline, to ponder a point, or for quick reference later.

Rule #1:

Develop a workable plan

Some of our dreams need a little money. This list is where we begin.

We need to have some idea of how much we need to save and how we will save it.

There may be part of you rebelling already. Relax! Of course you don't know the future! But it will serve you to *imagine* one scenario. The enemy of a good plan is the search for a perfect plan.

Make assumptions. Put them in writing.

Make assumptions, and then change them when you get better ideas or better information. Our goal is to enable these possibilities.

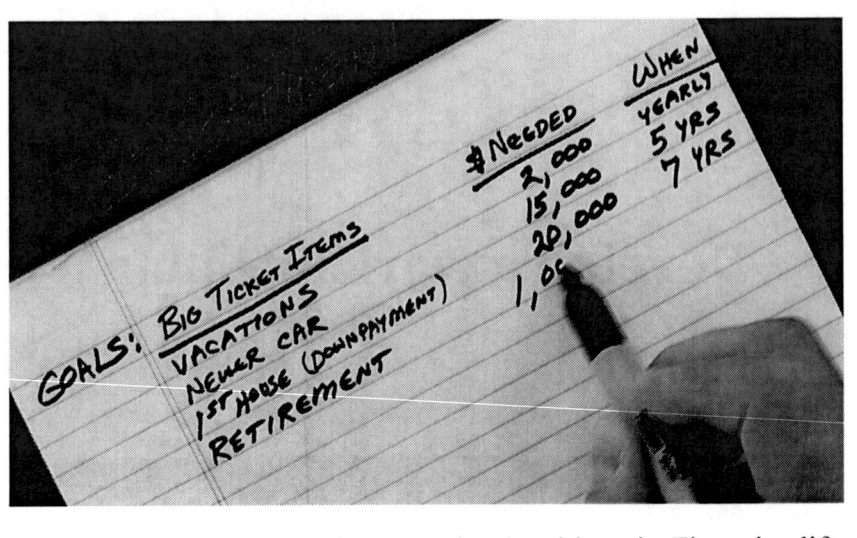

Let's pause here and consider some simple arithmetic. Financing life is about all of your dreams, but for most of you, saving for retirement will be the biggest item—by far!

Hopefully you have a long time to save for retirement, so I want to share two guidelines so that you can choose an appropriate goal for your investment plan.

If you reach retirement age in good health, there's a very good chance you, your spouse, or both of you, will enjoy 30 years of retirement. A good rule-of-thumb is that you'll need 25 times what you'll draw from your savings for 30 years of retirement. For example, you may wish to retire at age 65 on $60,000 a year. If you expect $20,000 a year from Social Security, then you'll need $40,000 a year from your savings. That means you'll need to save 25 x $40,000, or $1 million, to be fairly confident you won't run out of money if you live to age 95.

You might want half this, or twice this. It's a personal choice. This guideline does account for inflation and most stock market scenarios, but assumes your money is invested wisely, as we'll describe in later chapters.

Invest money you'll need soon very conservatively, like in a money market fund or a bank CD—definitely not the stock market. On the other hand, money you need beyond 10 years really should be invested in a portfolio of stocks and bonds, and that is what these ten rules will help you understand how to do correctly.

"But Rick," you say, "the stock market is *way* too volatile."

Correct! The next chart shows a history of annual returns of Large Company Stocks.

In any given year, the value might fall by half! Look what happened in 2008.

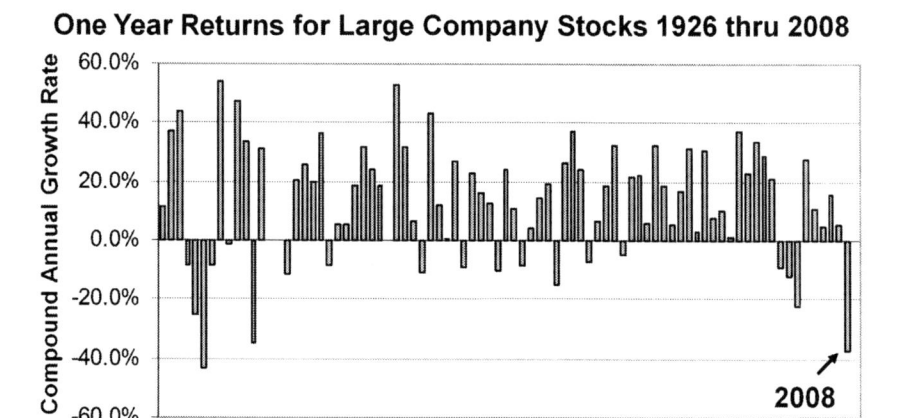

Do You See The Risk?
One Year Returns for Large Company Stocks 1926 thru 2008

Now let's look at the historical outcomes for holding stocks still longer. In the next chart, each bar represents the return after holding for 10 years. (See chapter footnotes.)

Sometimes people lose money after holding 10 years! (like 2008!)

But, most of the time stocks outperform an even bigger risk: inflation.

Now Where's The Risk?

Ten-Year Returns for Large Company Stocks 1926 thru 2008

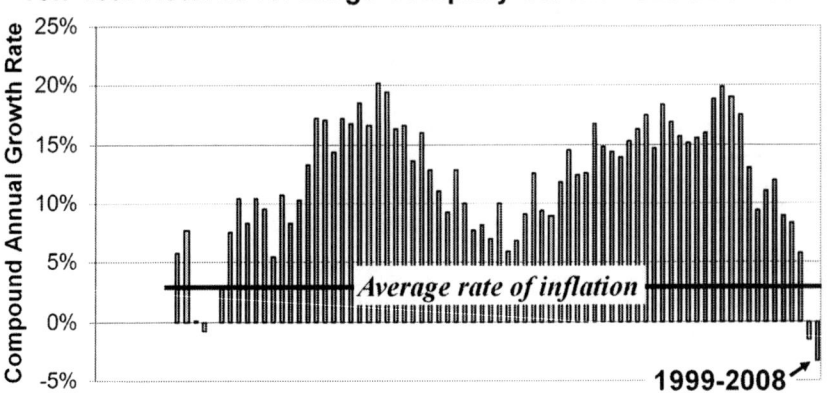

Invest to beat inflation

Your risk of losing your investment in the stock market is small over a long holding period. Your risk of losing the value of your investment due to inflation is much larger! This is why *you must invest* and you need an investment return bigger than inflation.

Suppose you plan to retire in 30 years and inflation is just average— every $1,000 you save today will be worth only $410!

Invest You Must
3% Inflation

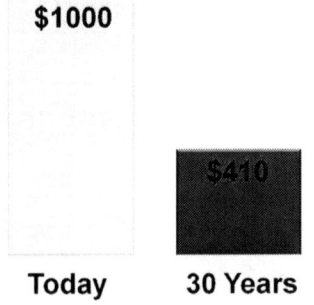

20

But wait, does this chart suggest we should own only stocks and hold them for a very long time—until you need that money? It's true our investments would grow, but we can't change the volatility of the stock market.

Remember, we saw that any given year your stock holdings might lose half of their value. We'll see in Rule #3 that each year we will want to gradually convert some of our stocks to bonds so that we don't hold too much risk by the time we need the money. One popular guideline we'll discuss later is to "own your age in bonds."

We're going to continue working on this plan all the way through Rule #10. Right now it probably looks like you are going to need a lot of money.

OK. So how much do you need to save? Here a short answer that works for most young adults: 5% of your gross paycheck for those big ticket items, and another 10% for your retirement.

And if you haven't already, you should use the very first money you save to establish a sound financial lifestyle before investing for the future. I have a separate video about this.

www.financinglife.org/start-with-sound-lifestyle/

Pay yourself first

If you get a paycheck, you already get a large slice withheld for various taxes. Here are some guidelines—details will vary state-to-state, individual-to-individual.

Our human behavior is that if we don't see it, we don't miss it. So *a time-proven strategy for saving is to pay yourself first* with that 15% automatically deposited.

Here's a balanced budget that works for many people. See how this works for you. It applies 45% of your gross income to your essential expenses that you *need*, and 15% to discretionary, or fun stuff.

Pay Yourself First

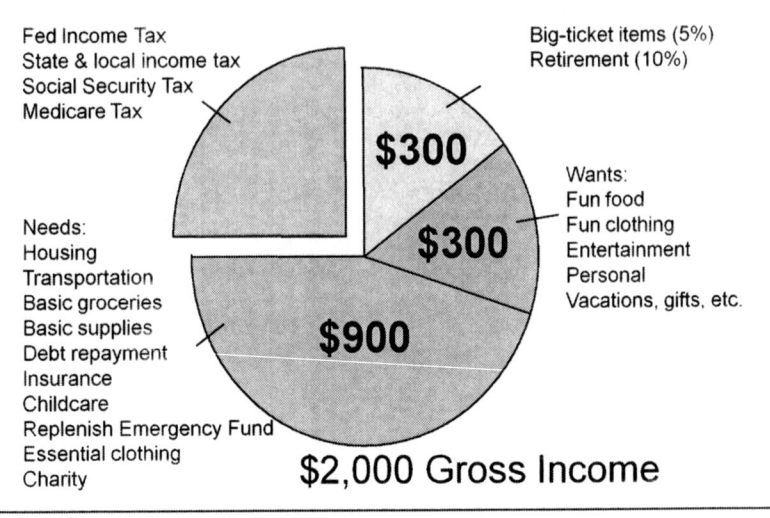

Fed Income Tax
State & local income tax
Social Security Tax
Medicare Tax

Big-ticket items (5%)
Retirement (10%)

Needs:
Housing
Transportation
Basic groceries
Basic supplies
Debt repayment
Insurance
Childcare
Replenish Emergency Fund
Essential clothing
Charity

Wants:
Fun food
Fun clothing
Entertainment
Personal
Vacations, gifts, etc.

$300

$300

$900

$2,000 Gross Income

This example budget saves 5% of gross income for near-term big-ticket items, and 10% for retirement. Initially, you might be thinking that you *need* everything you spend money on. Use these questions to get at your true foundation expenses:

1. Could you live in safety and dignity without this purchase?

2. If you lost your job, would you keep spending money on this?

3. Could you live without this purchase for six months?

If you withhold money from your paycheck to pay your taxes, and you pay yourself first with an automatic deposit for your long-term savings, then you don't need a complicated budget. You simply spend what you have left: one dollar for fun expenses for every three dollars you spend on the essentials you need.

Some of you might be thinking, "Hey, you're only young once. Maybe I should save 10% for big-ticket items, and only 5% for retirement." This is a tradeoff that only you can make.

Time is your friend. You'll see by example in our next rule how you can harness the power of compound interest by starting to save early.

Chapter Footnotes

Find this and other explanatory videos, smart tips, and links to useful resources at www.FinancingLife.org.

The story about risk and inflation is adapted from *The New Coffeehouse Investor: How to Build Wealth, Ignore Wall Street, and Get on with Your Life* by Bill Schultheis, 2009.

The budgeting basics are adapted from *On My Own Two Feet* by Manisha Thakor and Sharon Kedar, 2007.

Have a plan. Follow the plan, and you'll be surprised how successful you can be. Most people don't have a plan. That's why it's easy to beat most folks.

—Paul "Bear" Bryant

Rule #2:

Invest early and often

Example: two women, two stories

To illustrate the miracle of compound interest and the importance of starting to save early, I'd like you to consider two women, Tabitha and Tonya.

Tabitha

Accounting Job
$35,000 / yr

Saves $5,000 / yr for 10yr

Early Saver

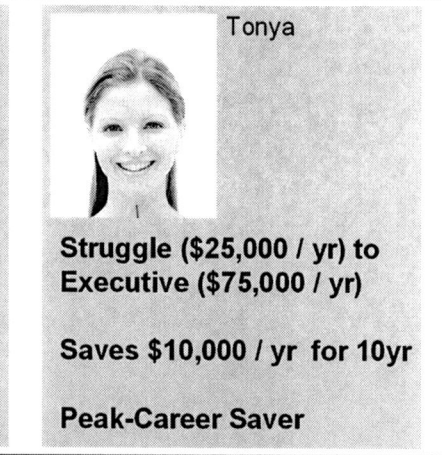

Tonya

Struggle ($25,000 / yr) to
Executive ($75,000 / yr)

Saves $10,000 / yr for 10yr

Peak-Career Saver

Tabitha graduated from college at age 22 and took a job with a starting salary of $35,000. Right away she began saving $5,000 a year for her retirement. She kept up this routine for ten years, saving a total of $50,000 out of her own pocket. Then, at age 32, she decided to quit her job and become a full-time mother. While she did not contribute another dollar to her savings, her existing savings continued to grow until she retired at age 65.

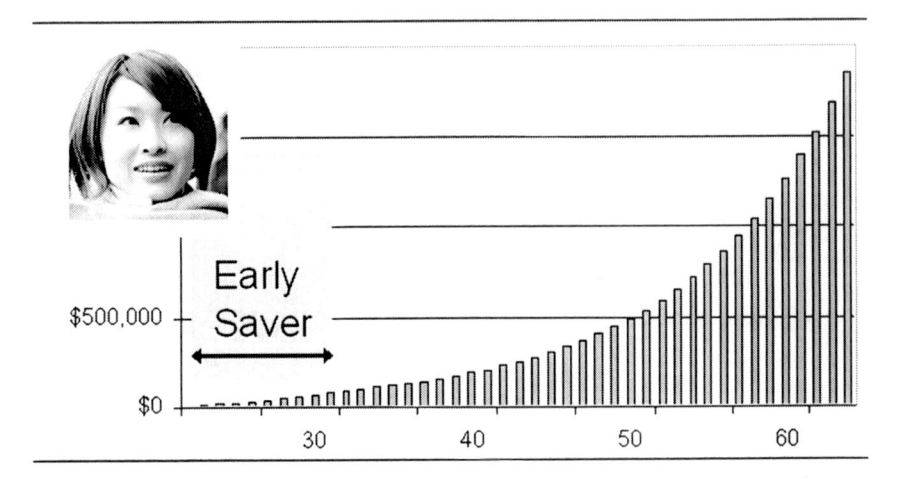

Early
Saver

$500,000

$0

30 40 50 60

Tonya, by contrast, took a lower paying job in an expensive part of the country. Her early years were a struggle and she saved nothing. But her career advanced with constant promotions. At age 40, she was a vice president making $75,000 a year. She finally felt that she was able to start saving for retirement, so she began putting away $10,000 a year. Tonya did this for ten years, saving a total of $100,000 out of her own pocket. At age 50, when her parents became very ill, she decided to quit her job to help take care of them so she stopped saving. Tonya's existing nest egg only got to grow for fifteen more years before she turned age 65.

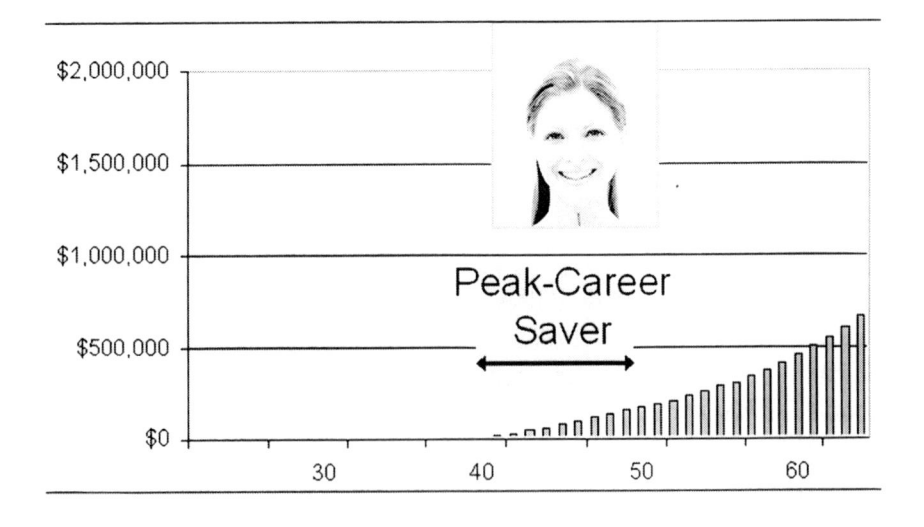

$2,000,000

$1,500,000

$1,000,000

Peak-Career
Saver

$500,000

$0

30 40 50 60

The million dollar difference!

While both women's investments grew at 10 percent per year, their nest eggs at age 65 were very different sizes. While Tabitha saved only half as much as Tonya out of her own pocket, she ended up with over $1 million more in her retirement.

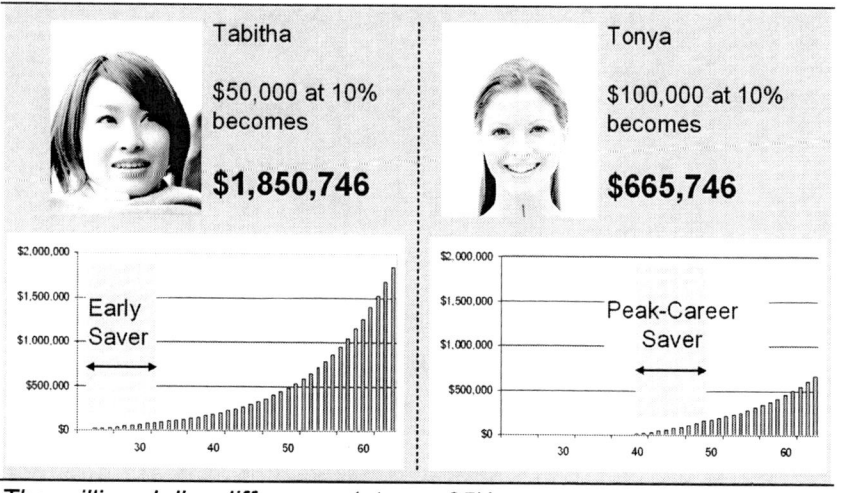

The million dollar difference (at age 65)!

The benefits of starting to save and invest early are simply enormous. Having time on your side and investing your hard-earned savings in a smart manner is the classic recipe for financial success.

Chapter Footnotes

Find this and other explanatory videos, smart tips, and links to useful resources at www.FinancingLife.org.

This storyline for this chapter is from *On My Own Two Feet*, by Manisha Thakor and Sharon Kedar, 2007, www.adamsmedia.com, pp 6-7, and is used with permission.

What do you consider to be humanity's greatest discovery?
"Compound interest."

   —Folklore attributes this quote to Albert Einstein
   but I have been unable to validate that.
   You get the point though.

Rule #3:

Never bear too much or too little risk

This chapter is about your most important decision—how much of your investment should be in stocks, and how much should be in bonds. This is all about managing risk. How much risk should you take? And how, exactly, do you go about that?

Variability measures risk

There are safe places to put your money and it might grow like this.

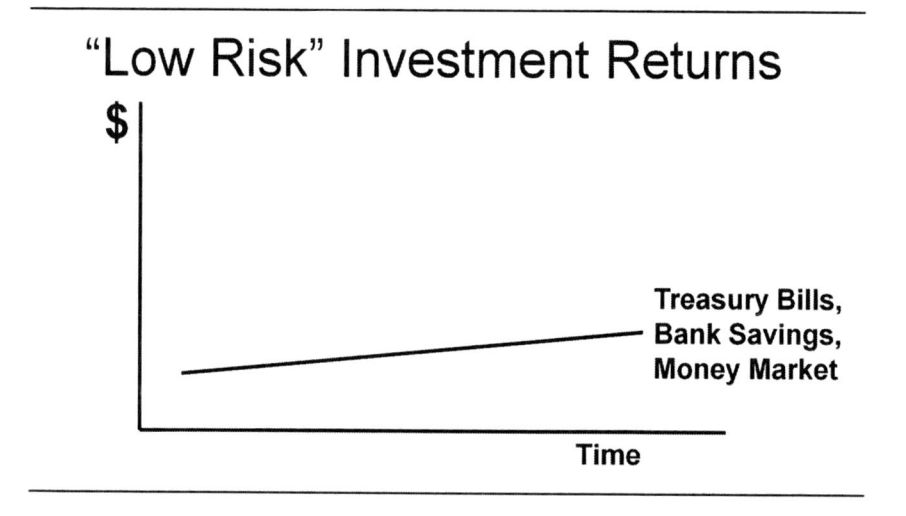

"Low Risk" Investment Returns

After-taxes, it's not likely to keep up with inflation. You have many choices to earn a higher return but all are less predictable, which means that the money might not be there when you need it. So variability of the return is one good measure of risk.

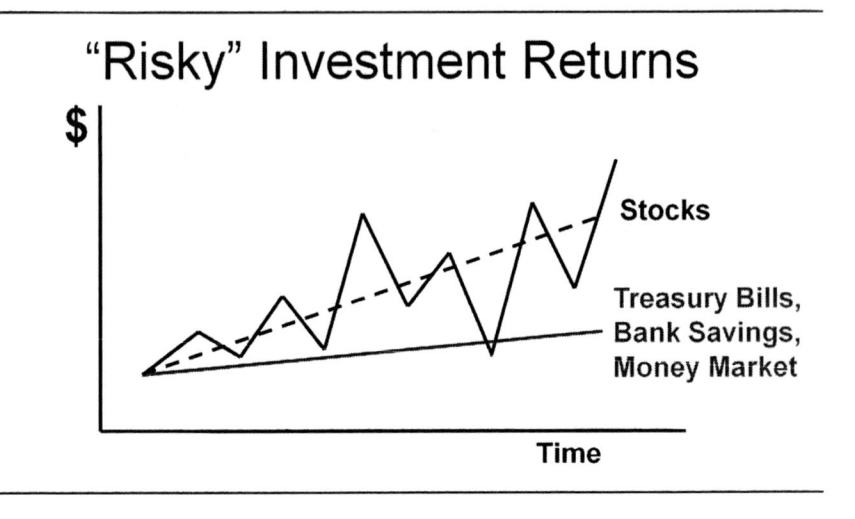

"Risky" Investment Returns

Expect higher returns for riskier investments

If we plot that risk, or variability, with the return on investment, our risk-free alternatives go on the left. Treasury bonds are not risk-free because their value varies with the current interest rate. Stocks have a high risk and return.

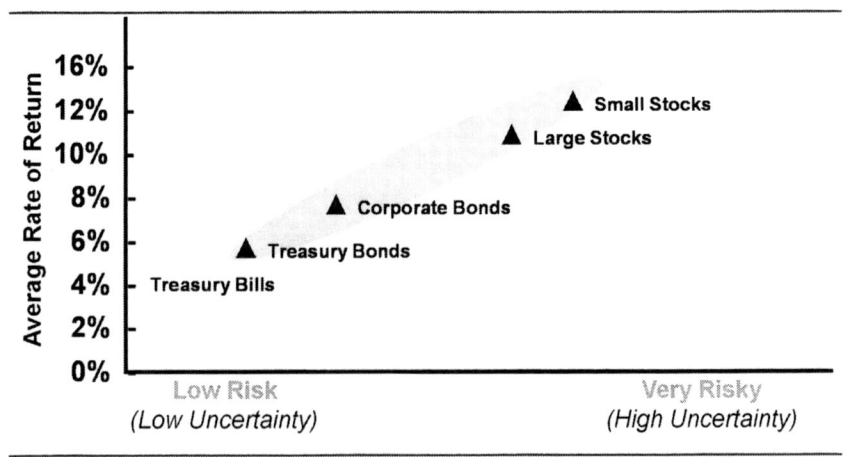

The market provides higher expected returns for riskier investments.

Distilled to its essence, investing is about earning a return in exchange for shouldering risk. Here's the catch that many investors miss: *this is only true for diversified portfolios.*

Dilute specific-company risk

For instance, you could buy the S&P 500 which is a low-cost benchmark index of the 500 largest companies. But if you were to pick any one company, your risk would be far greater—even any five of them, or ten, or twenty. Examples of this specific company risk that can be diversified away might be the departure of a key executive, the outcome of an important court case, or employees going on strike.

Dilute specific-company risk. The market does not compensate you for holding this risk since it can be eliminated by owning many companies.

Your total risk includes market-risk (events that move the whole market) plus specific-company risk (like we described above). Specific-company risk can be eliminated by using mutual funds which own many companies. Market-risk cannot.

It is usually unwise to speculate in specific companies unless you have exceptional information about what you are investing in (rare). If you wish a higher expected return than the S&P 500 largest companies, choose an index fund in an asset class which has both higher risk and higher expected return—like small company stocks.

Don't put all your eggs in one basket is the popular cliché. You simply don't get rewarded for the risk you are taking. It moves you from investing, to speculating. Author William Bernstein noted: "*Concentrating your portfolio in a few stocks maximizes your chances of getting rich. Unfortunately, it also maximizes your chance of becoming poor.*"[1]

Bonds are the other essential ingredient because they behave differently than stocks. So you need to learn about both of these. The ratio of stocks to bonds you own is your key lever that controls your risk.

Ability, willingness, and need for risk

There is no "right" portfolio, but there is one that is best for *you*—one that carries the appropriate level of risk. In order to determine what that is, investing expert Larry Swedroe encourages you to consider *your ability, willingness, and need to take risk.*[2]

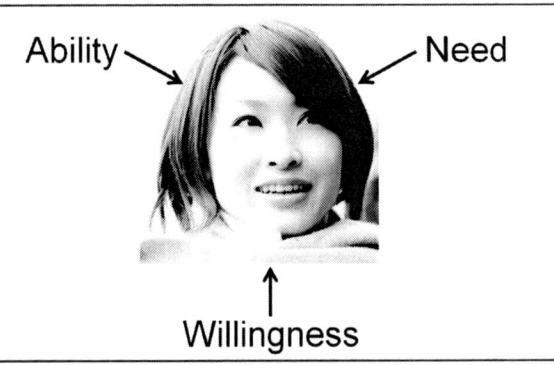

You need to consider all three factors to determine the level of risk that is appropriate for your long-term investments.

Your *ability to take risk* is determined by your investment horizon and the stability of your income. At the beginning of this series, you considered how much money you needed for your goals and when. The longer you have, the better you can weather the inevitable market downturns. If you need the money in a few years, you should keep it out of the stock market. Money that you won't need for 10 or 20 years might be best in stocks. Also, the more stable your job, the greater your ability to handle the risks of owning stocks.

Nick is a 30 year-old who's been saving aggressively for eight years. He is saving half of his money for a new house in a few years and the other half is for his retirement. It is important for him to keep the risk out of his money that he might need in the short-term. His retirement investments might be primarily in the stock market—depending on these other considerations.

Next, consider your *willingness to take risk*. As we saw before, the stock market has high long-term returns, but in the short term it is very volatile. Any year your stock could lose half its value. The key thing is how you will behave during the next recession. If you sell when the market is low—you do yourself a real disservice. You are better off starting with a number you can live with and then stick to it!

Finally, your *need to take risk* is determined by your financial goals and what rate of return is required to achieve them.

Now, if you are 40 years old, very risk averse and haven't started to save for your retirement yet, then your willingness to take risk might conflict with your financial needs. You will need to earn more, save more, retire later, acquire the temperament to carry more risk (more stocks), or some combination.

Own your age in bonds?

If you are having trouble choosing what level is right for you, I will tell you that I think a good starting place is the advice to *own your age in bonds*. So, a 25-year old might own 25% bonds and 75% stocks, gradually changing these by 1% every birthday.

"Own Your Age in Bonds"

Use your age to decide percentage of portfolio value to own in bonds.

Examples:

Age 25: | $3,000 in stocks | $1,000 |

Age 50: | $300,000 in stocks | $300,000 in bonds |

Age 75: | $200,000 | $600,000 in bonds |

Variation: Own (Age-10) in Bonds

In this example, your portfolio value increases with age, and the percentage of the portfolio value invested in bonds increases by 1% every birthday (age 25 = 25%). Surprisingly, the distinction between these two is much less important than choosing something appropriate and then *sticking to it*.

Once the stocks and bonds decision is made, you can move on to the decision on what types of mutual funds you'll want to own.

Chapter Footnotes

Find this and other explanatory videos, smart tips, and links to useful resources at www.FinancingLife.org.

(1) *The Four Pillars of Investing: Lessons for Building a Winning Portfolio*, William Bernstein, 2002, p.101.

(2) An excellent discussion about ability, willingness, and need to take risk is in *The Successful Investor Today: 14 Simple Truths You Must Know When You Invest*, by Larry E. Swedroe, 2003, pp 222-225.

Rule #4:

Diversify

Previously, we saw how owning many stocks eliminated "specific company risk." Now we are going to see that it is not enough to simply own hundreds of companies. You'll learn the great advantage of owning poorly correlated assets. This part is truly cool! *Magical.*

Low correlation provides a "free lunch"

To show you, let's imagine two companies: Bathing Suits Inc. and National Umbrella Company. A rainy year means sales at the Bathing Suit company fall but the umbrella company does well. In a sunny year, the bathing suit company does well and the sales of umbrellas fall.

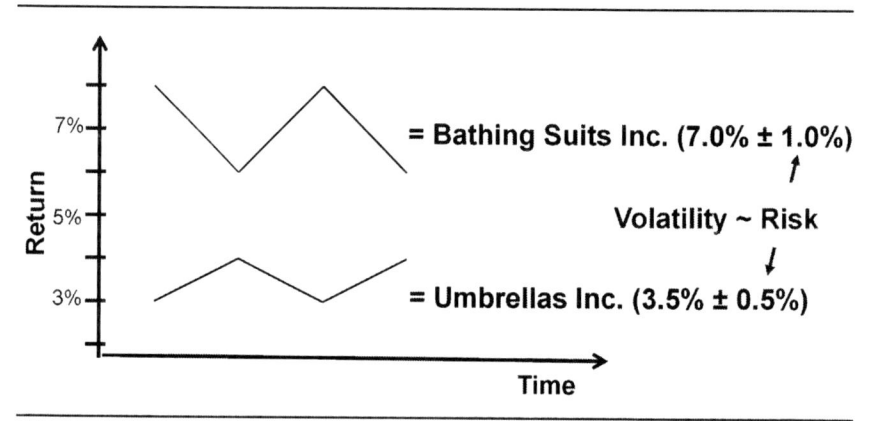

Ideal example! Companies' returns move in opposite directions.

The price of these company stocks move in opposite directions so they are negatively correlated. The Bathing Suit company is more volatile because the total annual return has an average value of 7.0% but varies by plus or minus 1.0%. This is both higher return and higher risk than the umbrella company which has an average return of 3.5% plus or minus 0.5%.

This is the magical part. Look what happens if you invest 2/3 of your money in the umbrella company and 1/3 in the bathing suit company. WOW! Adding some of the more volatile company to your portfolio not only increases the average return, but it lowers the variability (or risk). Pretty much a free lunch!

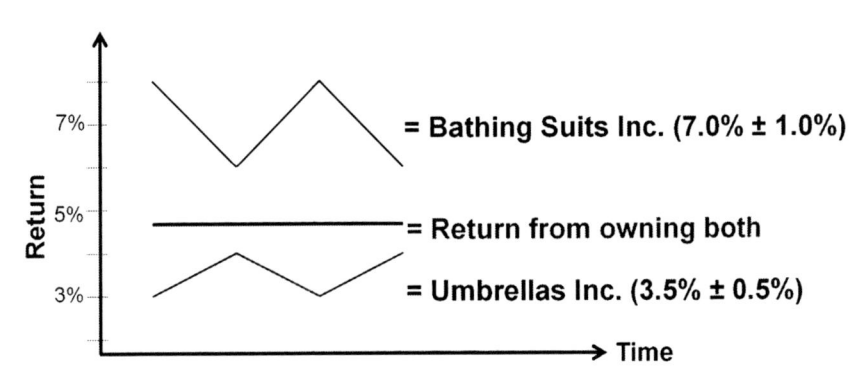

Benefits of Low Correlation

WOW! *Adding a More Volatile asset can increase return and lower risk!*

In this example, owning some of both reduces risk (volatility) to zero

Next, see what it looks like on a risk-return chart. The Bathing Suit Company is in the upper right with twice the expected risk and return as the umbrella company. If you owned 100% of the umbrella company you'd be left and lower (less risk, less return). Now if you gradually invest part of your portfolio in the more risky Bathing Suit Company, your returns increase as you expected, but your risk, as measured by the variability of that return, actually decreases. Owning both is superior to only owning either of the companies.

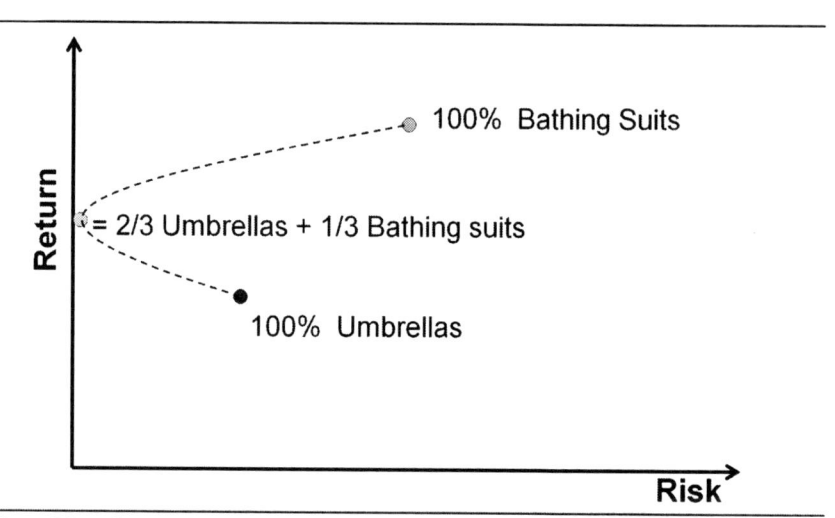

Combinations of ownership can be anywhere along dotted line.

This is an important, and surprising, point. In the previous rule, we saw how different types of investments are distributed along a line that extends up to the right on a Risk-Return chart. This is because investors demand higher expected-returns in exchange for shouldering more risk. But now we see that when you can combine poorly correlated assets, you get the desirable situation where adding a more volatile asset can increase expected returns and lower risk.

Everyone should own some bonds

Negatively correlated stocks move in opposite directions or, more precisely: one tends to produce returns above its average when the other tends to produce returns below its average. These are hard to find and still achieve diversified investments, so we look for the next best thing: poorly correlated investments. For instance, recall that the price of bonds move in the opposite direction of interest rates. But interest rates don't impact the sales of bathing suits and umbrellas, and the weather doesn't impact the price of bonds. So we pretty generally say that the stock market and Treasury Bonds are nearly uncorrelated and we get this same magical benefit. Adding a little of the stock market to an all-bond portfolio has historically increased the expected returns and decreased the volatility (risk). Going forward, we may expect something similar, but caution: correlations can change when viewed over different timeframes.

37

Stocks Zig when Bonds Zag!

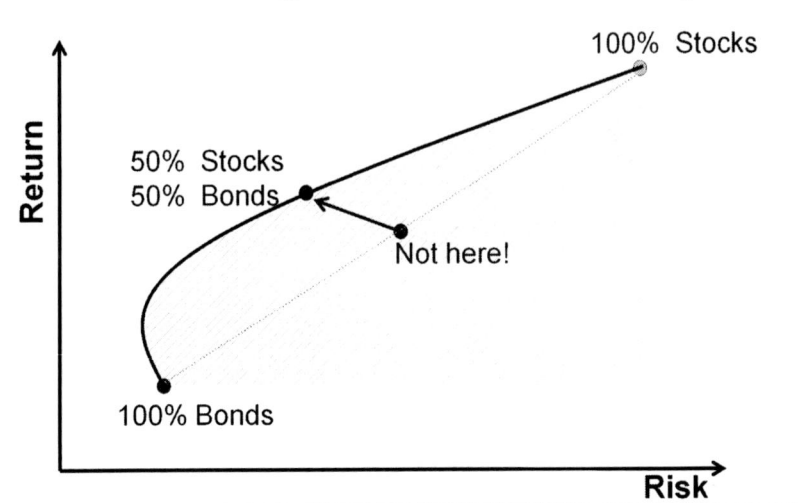

This is precisely how it works in the real world. Say you determined that 50% stocks and 50% bonds was the right level of risk for you. Instead of being halfway between like you might expect in the diagram above, the fact that stocks are poorly correlated with bonds puts you up in a region with higher expected return and lower risk. This is terrific![1]

What else can we do? If we take a closer look at stocks, we find out that the primary factors that determine the outcome of stock investments in the long-term are: size of the companies, whether they are a glamorous growth company or a less glamorous value company, and then what region of the world it is in.[2]

The companies in the S&P 500 are so huge that this famous benchmark index is a good approximation of the entire US Stock Market. These 500 companies encompass both large Value and large Growth companies. Alternatively, choose a Total US Stock Market Index fund to further diversify with smaller companies and to now own a portion of several thousand companies!

Stocks in foreign companies are even less correlated[3] with the US stock market, but are more expensive to own and have added volatility (risk) from currency exchange fluctuations if the assets are unhedged. Many investors make 1/4 to 1/2 of their total stock percentage a broad international stock index fund.

You started a plan with goals and a saving routine—fully knowing that you may change it as life happens. In the last chapter, you chose an appropriate level of stocks and bonds that matched your ability, willingness, and need to take risk. That's always your most important decision. Now you can see how broadly-diversified index funds are perfect for your target stock allocations.

Bonds are much simpler. You can keep the risk out of bonds by keeping them short- to intermediate-term and very high quality. To diversify against inflation it is popular to make half of them US Treasury bonds, called "TIPS", for Treasury Inflation-Protected Securities. High-quality bonds also differ from high-yield bonds in that they are less correlated with the stock market—important to get that "magical" benefit known as the Modern Portfolio Theory advantage.

Building an outstanding portfolio doesn't have to be complicated at all!

Chapter Footnotes

Find this and other explanatory videos, smart tips, and links to useful resources at www.FinancingLife.org.

(1) The benefits of poorly correlated assets is a small portion of Modern Portfolio Theory for which several economists won the Nobel Prize. This particular chart of stocks and bonds is a simplification of one that appears in *All About Asset Allocation: The Easy Way to Get Started*, by Richard A. Ferri, 2006, p.45.

(2) The importance of company size and style (growth vs value) for explaining the differences in returns of diversified portfolios is known today as the Fama-French Three Factor Model.

(3) The correlation of various asset classes to the S&P 500 Index is listed in *The Only Guide To A Winning Investment Strategy You'll Ever Need*, 2005, by Larry E. Swedroe, p 144.

If you are not a professional investor, if your goal is not to manage money in such a way that you get a significantly better return than world, then I believe in extreme diversification.

I believe that 98 or 99 percent — maybe more than 99 percent — of people who invest should extensively diversify and not trade. That leads them to an index fund with very low costs.

All they're going to do is own a part of America. They've made a decision that owning a part of America is worthwhile. I don't quarrel with that at all — that is the way they should approach it.

—Warren Buffett

Listen to him yourself.
Skip to the 1:12 mark of the following online video: Warren Buffet explains to MBA students at the University of Florida why he believes index funds are the best choice for most investors.
http://www.youtube.com/watch?v=P-PobeU4Ox0

Rule #5:

Never try to time the market

Imagine this: You've invested in a stock, or a fund, and its value has plummeted to half of what it was worth a year ago, with no end in sight. You hate to lose money! Should you sell to prevent further loss?

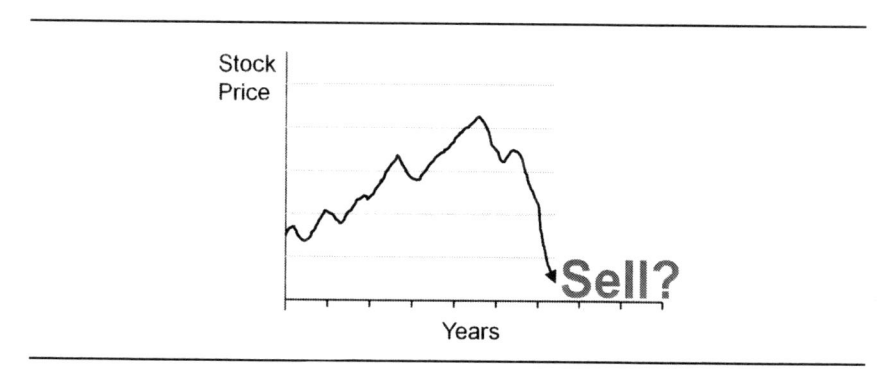

Or, perhaps the market's been rising and you are wondering whether you are missing the boat and should be owning the current winner?

These are examples of trying to beat the market using timing. It's a loser's game. It is at least very difficult, if not impossible, to succeed at market timing over the long-run.

It turns out that investor money flows into stock funds after good performance, and goes out when bad performance follows. Investors chasing performance are typically too late.

Expenses and emotion-driven selling

For a recent 25-year period, John Bogle found that the vast majority of investors earned 5% less than the overall stock market return. Over half of this gap was from market timing, the rest unnecessary costs.[1]

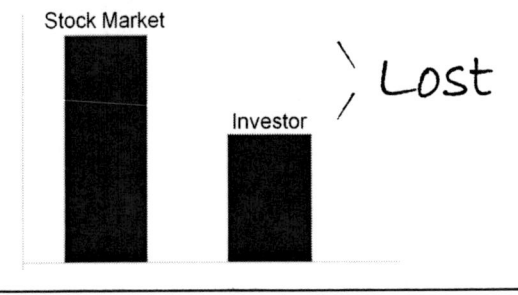

Return on Investment

The average investor earns far less than the stock market average. Why? Almost half is lost to expenses; balance from investor behavior (timing).

It's simple to achieve the market return because you can buy a single mutual fund that owns all publicly held companies for a low cost. But, it's only easy if you have a plan that matches your ability, willingness, and need to take risk, then you stick to it and weather all the sales efforts that are targeted at you.

To make money from stocks and bonds, it is important to acknowledge that you are investing in companies, either by becoming a lender to them, through holding a company's bond, or by becoming a partner with them, through buying a company's stock. We collectively buy and hold these shares for the long term, sharing the wealth all these companies generate through their growth, resourcefulness, and innovation. And we, collectively, all earn the market return.

Before expenses, the winners equal the losers

But within this pool of shareholders, there is short-term trading between investors. And *for every dollar that outperforms the market*

42

return, there is a dollar of underperformance. The huge financial services industry is very adept at convincing you that they can help you get better returns than the market so that you'll watch their channel, purchase their newsletter, or invest in their fund. But in the end, the amount of over-performance (which you'll hear a lot about) must equal the amount of underperformance (which you won't hear about) because the market return is the average.

Larry Swedroe points out that most investors think they are competing against you and me. But about 90% of stock trades are by institutional investors. You are not buying from, or selling to, your neighbor next door whom you may be smarter than, but these institutional investors who are focused on this full-time with great resources. Do you think you are going to outperform institutional investors? Do you think this is Lake Wobegon where everybody is above average?

The next chapter will help you distinguish a good fund from a lousy one.

Attempting to predict the future direction of the market is only the first of the two common timing mistakes.

The strong lure to buy recent performance

It's also incredibly tempting to invest in the most recent, top performing categories of stocks and bonds.

Individual asset categories, like small cap growth companies or real estate companies, are constantly moving between being the year's top performer to being the year's worst performer. This is particularly obvious at a glance when viewed in color in what is sometimes called the periodic table of investment returns. The following picture is an excerpt of what you'll see if you follow the footnote link to Russell Investments.[2]

	2006	2007	2008	2009	2010
BEST PERFORMANCE	REAL ESTATE 35.06	LARGE CAP GROWTH 11.81	BONDS 5.24	LARGE CAP GROWTH 37.21	SMALL CAP GROWTH 29.09
	INT'L 26.86	INT'L 11.63	SMALL CAP VALUE -28.92	SMALL CAP GROWTH 34.47	REAL ESTATE 27.95
	SMALL CAP VALUE 23.48	SMALL CAP GROWTH 7.05	SMALL CAP -33.79	INT'L 32.46	SMALL CAP 26.85
	LARGE CAP VALUE 22.25	BONDS 6.97	LARGE CAP VALUE -36.85	LARGE CAP 28.43	SMALL CAP VALUE 24.50
	SMALL CAP 18.37	LARGE CAP 5.77	LARGE CAP -37.60	REAL ESTATE 27.99	LARGE CAP GROWTH 16.71
	LARGE CAP 15.46	LARGE CAP VALUE -0.17	REAL ESTATE -37.73	SMALL CAP 27.17	LARGE CAP 16.10
	SMALL CAP GROWTH 13.35	SMALL CAP -1.57	LARGE CAP GROWTH -38.44	SMALL CAP VALUE 20.58	LARGE CAP VALUE 15.51
	LARGE CAP GROWTH 9.07	SMALL CAP VALUE -9.78	SMALL CAP GROWTH -38.54	LARGE CAP VALUE 19.69	INT'L 8.21
WEAKEST PERFORMANCE	BONDS 4.33	REAL ESTATE -15.69	INT'L -43.06	BONDS 5.93	BONDS 6.54

I circled "small cap growth" performance. Do you see how yesterday's winners are often tomorrow's losers? Predictions here are futile. Now *you* circle "real estate" for each year. Do you see the mistake of investing in yesterday's top performers?

John Bogle warns, "Don't think you know more than the market. Nobody does."[3] Winning strategies buy and hold a portion of all of the nation's publicly held businesses at a very low cost. By doing so you are guaranteed to capture almost the entire return that they generate in the form of dividends and earnings growth.[4]

Example: scheduled investments and rebalancing

Here's a short example. Henry is saving for his retirement in 30 years. He chooses to own his age in bonds which means, this year, 35% of his retirement savings are allocated to bonds, and 65% are allocated to a fund that owns the entire stock market. He rebalances every birthday so very gradually his percentage of bonds increases. Appendix E shows an example of rebalancing.

Example: Henry (age 35)

Saves $400 /month for retirement in 30 years

Bonds	Stocks	
35%	65%	Rebalance annually

Now, does he hesitate after every paycheck and consider whether stocks might be cheaper to buy tomorrow? No. He set up his purchases to occur automatically and avoids that first timing mistake.

Does he ever consider which companies (or mutual funds) are doing best this month? Nope. By simply buying a small piece of the whole market, he gets to own them all and avoids that second timing mistake.

How 'bout rebalancing every birthday: is that "market timing"? No again. It's an example of having a plan and sticking to it.

Chapter Footnotes

Find this and other explanatory videos, smart tips, and links to useful resources at www.FinancingLife.org.

(1) "Yes, during the past 25 years, while the stock market index fund was providing an annual return of 12.3 percent and the average equity fund was earning an annual return of 10.0 percent, the average fund investor was earning only 7.3 percent a year." *The Little Book of Common Sense Investing: The Only Way to Guarantee Your Fair Share of Stock Market Returns*, by John C. Bogle, 2007, p.51.

(2) Find two alternative views of a periodic table of investment returns in color, more detail, and over 15-20 year timeframes:

www.callan.com/research/download/?file=periodic%2Ffree%2F457.pdf

www.russell.com/us/documents/syndication/value_of_diversification_004000579.pdf

(3) John C. Bogle, *Common Sense on Mutual Funds: New Imperatives for the Intelligent Investor*, 1999.

(4) John C. Bogle, *The Little Book of Common Sense Investing: The Only Way to Guarantee Your Fair Share of Stock Market Returns*, p.xi.

Rule #6:

Use index funds when possible

In prior chapters we've established that you'll want both stocks and bonds, from many, diversified companies, and that you need to avoid market timing.

Mutual funds are definitely the convenient way to invest in hundreds, or even thousands, of diverse companies. So, how do we recognize a good mutual fund from a bad one?

Misleading rankings based on recent performance

This is where our instincts get us in trouble. We are comfortable using rating systems to guide our other purchases. So most people are attracted to mutual funds rated four or five stars by Morningstar®.

Here's an actively-managed fund that tries to beat the market return, and a passively-managed fund that attempts to match the market return.

	Typical Morningstar Rating
Aggressive Stock Fund	★ ★ ★ ★ ★
Total Stock Market Index Fund	★ ★ ★

A key point that I want you to understand is that these rankings are based on past performance so have very little relevance![1]

Here's why. Remember, "the Market" is the collection of all stocks, all investors. So for every active manager who beats the average market return, another loses by the same amount. Unfortunately, the only way to profit from those winning funds is to know the winners in advance, which is impossible to know.[2]

There are a variety of reasons why the winners don't enjoy persistent success. Sometimes success attracts an over-whelming amount of new money to a fund. Sometimes the manager's style of investing goes out of favor. And sometimes the managers were never good, just lucky, and their luck runs out.[3]

Why index funds must beat active funds

In contrast, index funds are passively managed and can be very low cost. An index fund simply owns all the stocks that make up an asset category, or in this case, all asset categories. The goal is not to beat the market, but to match the market return as measured by a benchmark index. For instance, the S&P 500 is a benchmark index for the 500 largest companies in the United States. A different, broader index benchmarks the entire stock market.

Active Funds	Index Funds
• Beat Market (try)	• Match Market
• Expensive (1-3% /yr)	• Low Cost (0.1% /yr)

Active funds require a talented staff and excellent insightful research to try to predict which companies will outperform tomorrow, and frequent trading. All these expenses get paid first; investors just get what is left.

"We get to keep, precisely what we don't pay for!"

Market Return - Investor's Costs = Investor's Return

You want the lowest possible costs!

So, to beat the market after subtracting these costs is very challenging.

Probability of an active equity fund beating the market

Only 37% of active funds beat the market every year.[4,5] But there is little persistence, and within five years, the number of winners has dropped to 25%. Over a period of 10 years, a mere 15% of the actively managed funds beat the "market return," which is what you would get if you had invested in a low-cost, highly-diversified index fund.

Probability of an Active Equity Fund Beating the Market

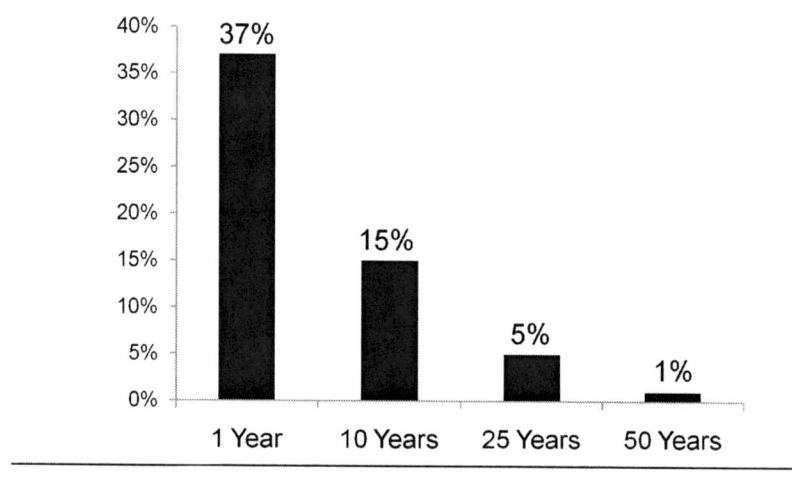

Bill Schultheis calls this dismal performance "*Wall Street's Best Kept Secret.*"[6] It illustrates that you have a low probability of beating the market, and the odds get worse with time. Plus remember, it is impossible to choose the winners in advance. Bill also invented an instructive game called Outfox-the-Box in his book *The New Coffeehouse Investor*.

Outfox-the-Box (with clairvoyance)

Imagine that you want to invest $10,000 and there are only nine mutual funds in the world.[7] Eight of them are active funds with an annual cost of 2%. One of them is a low-cost index fund that closely tracks the overall market return.

Nine Funds. Which to Choose?

Cost of Active Funds: 2.00% per year
Cost of Index Fund: 0.1% per year

Active #1	Active #2	Active #3
Active #8	Index #9	Active #4
Active #7	Active #6	Active #5

You are clairvoyant and can foresee that you have two out of eight chances of outperforming the market over the next five years (recall the 25% probability), and you know the odds will decline further with time.

The next picture illustrates this with numbers. Four active funds beat the market before expenses—they are shaded. Only two active funds beat the market after expenses—the two shaded in right-hand column. The reward for such long odds is an extra $2,000 or $4,000. But the average return from all the active funds is less than the market return by $1,300—the same as the amount subtracted for expenses.

Fund	Gross Return	-	Expenses	=	Investor Return
#1 (active):	$10,900	-	$1,300	=	$ 9,600
#2 (active):	$12,900	-	$1,300	=	$11,600
#3 (active):	$15,400	-	$1,300	=	$14,100
#4 (active):	$15,900	-	$1,300	=	$14,600
#5 (index):	$16,100	-	$ 100	=	$16,000
#6 (active)	$16,300	-	$1,300	=	$15,000
#7 (active)	$16,800	-	$1,300	=	$15,500
#8 (active)	$19,300	-	$1,300	=	$18,000
#9 (active)	$21,300	-	$1,300	=	$20,000

Before costs, odds of winning are 50/50. Some active funds will beat the market average, but the returns of the other active funds will be lower by the same amount. That's the definition of the market average—which index funds seek to match. After costs, the odds of beating the market drop dramatically. The odds after five years drop to roughly two of eight active funds.

You have this information, so you further notice that if it wasn't for those expenses, four of the active funds would beat the market, and four would not. And, averaged together, the eight active funds would have achieved the market return. After all, that's what the market return is, by definition. You can know the odds. You can know the arithmetic. But you can't know in advance which funds are going to outperform so cover them up. You are going to have to guess. Do you want to invest in the index fund and get the average market return, or do you want to try to beat the market with one of the active funds. And, if so which one?

Congratulations if you chose the index fund. It shows that you are a rational, risk-averse investor.

Now, do you agree with me that rankings based on past performance might be a little misleading? Five stars for a fund that outperformed recently, but has a very low chance of outperforming over the next ten years? And, of course the index fund is only rated mid-pack: *It can't outperform the market; it tracks the market!*

The best predictive measures of a fund's future performance are its costs and how closely it tracks the market.[8] Now, do you think that you don't have costs because you only buy "no load" funds? If so, don't miss the next chapter.

Chapter Footnotes

Find this and other explanatory videos, smart tips, and links to useful resources at www.FinancingLife.org.

(1) It is *investors* who misuse the fund rankings. Morningstar® clearly describes what the rankings are based on and explain that they "shouldn't be considered buy or sell signals." And yet we do. http://corporate.morningstar.com/us/documents/methodologydocu ments/factsheets/morningstarratingforfunds_factsheet.pdf

(2) *The Arithmetic of Active Management*, William F. Sharpe http://www.stanford.edu/~wfsharpe/art/active/active.htm

(3) *All About Index Funds*, by Richard A Ferri, 2nd Edition, McGraw-Hill, 2007, p.26. Used with permission.

(4) *All About Index Funds*, by Richard A Ferri, 2nd Edition, McGraw-Hill, 2007, p.25. Used with permission

(5) *The Case for Indexing*, Vanguard, February 2011 https://institutional.vanguard.com/iwe/pdf/ICRPI.pdf

(6) *The Coffeehouse Investor: How to Build Wealth, Ignore Wall Street, And Get On With Your Life* by Bill Schultheis, p.65.

(7) This "outfox the box" game was originally presented by Bill Schultheis in his delightful little book, *The Coffeehouse Investor: How to Build Wealth, Ignore Wall Street, And Get On With Your Life* (Palouse Press, 2005). I added details to make this example consistent with typical fund expenses, and consistent with the odds of beating the market in five years. Used with permission.

(8) *The Little Book of Common Sense Investing: The Only Way to Guarantee Your Fair Share of Stock Market Returns*, by John C. Bogle, John Wiley & Sons, Inc., 2007, p. 189.

Rule #7:

Keep costs low

The return-on-investment for vast majority of investors is substantially worse than the stock market as a whole.

Two chapters ago we looked at how the behavior of market timing, or trying to pick specific stocks or funds, accounts for about half of this gap. The rest we give away as costs.[1]

Last chapter we introduced the idea that the best and least expensive way to buy the whole stock market is with index funds. This is because the costs of actively managed funds make them very unlikely to beat the total market index funds.

Only a small percentage of active funds outperform the total stock market index funds, and you can't choose them in advance. Moreover, that probability gets lower every year.[2]

Three flavors of mutual fund costs

Three costs that I want you to be very aware of are sales charges, operating expenses, and taxes.

Pay Attention To Costs
1. Sales Charges
2. Operating Expenses
3. Income Taxes

A sales charge (or, "load") on purchases is exactly what you'd expect. If there's a 5% sales charge, you write a check for $10,000 but only $9,500 gets invested because $500 goes to the salesman. Sometimes a back-end sales load is deducted from the redemption proceeds instead.

Too often, brokers or commissioned agents actually think they are helping you by recommending to you recent top-performing actively-managed funds. This is bad advice! It makes other people wealthy instead of you.

When you can, buy from one of the big discount brokerage houses and look for low-cost, highly-diversified index funds without these sales fees. These kind of funds are called no-load funds, or marked NTF for "No Transaction Fee", although there might be a footnote that restricts this to online purchases that are held longer than some number of months.

Now here is the important number that I want you to remember. The annual recurring management fee is usually called *expense ratio*. It's a funny term that you need to remember. It is the percentage of a mutual fund's assets that the investment firm incurs for all of its regular operating costs.

Recurring Mutual Fund Costs

Expense Ratio   +   Additional

- Management Fees
- Distribution Expenses
- Custodial, Legal, Admin

- Brokerage Commissions
- Bid-Offer Spreads
- Market Impact Costs
- Soft-Dollar Arrangements

Expense Ratios

2.0%
1.5% ⎫
         ⎬ Average
1.0% ⎭
0.5% ⎴ Very Good
0.0% ⎠ Excellent!

The cost of owning mutual funds is not limited to their respective expense ratios. Transaction costs and market spreads are examples of additional costs a fund incurs every time it buys or sells a security. I only mention them because frequent trading is part of the reason that actively managed mutual funds underperform the total stock market.[3]

Here's an example: the Total Stock Market Index Fund offered by Vanguard. We can click on the Fees tab to find the expense ratio is 0.07% for this particular fund. All funds must publish this. If our total investment was only $10,000 then we would pay only $7 per year. This is excellent. They subtract that first and investors get what is left.

More on why investors underperform the Market

Earlier we saw how ill-timed market decisions cause undisciplined buying and selling. This keeps individuals from even achieving the returns of average funds. Now our attention is focused on the costs that keep these active funds from achieving the returns of index funds—which closely approximate the average returns of the whole market without any fund expenses.

Surprise! The returns actually earned by average investors are far less than the Market return. They are on the right side of this chart drawn from data in John Bogle's book.[4]

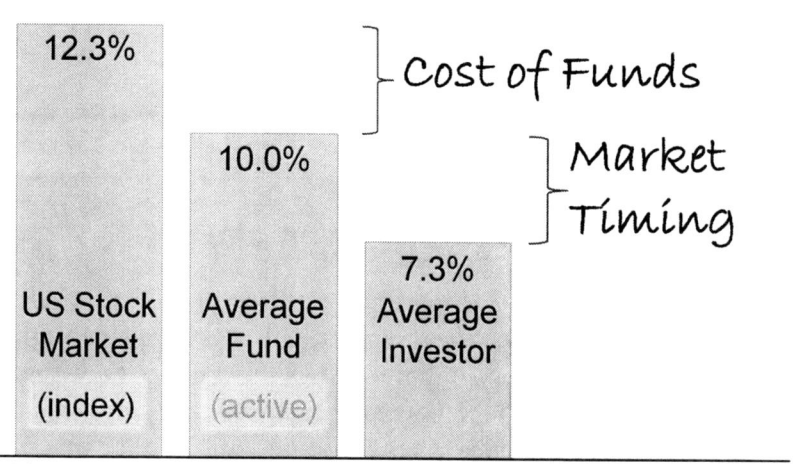

Most investors earn far less than the market (without knowing it?).

With mutual funds, it's not: "You get what you pay for."

"The grim irony of investing, then, is that we investors as a group not only don't get what we pay for. We get precisely what we *don't* pay for. *So if we pay nothing, we get everything.* It's only common sense."[5,6]

What you pay as expenses comes directly out of your pocket. The fund in this example, Total Stock Market Index Fund (VTSAX), has no sales charges. There is an annual fee for the account, but they point out ways to avoid these as well.

Little percentages make a BIG difference

These *little percentages make a big difference*! Here is a portion of a screenshot from the Vanguard website for that mutual fund where they show us how their expense ratio compares with the industry and how, if reinvested, that could be worth nearly $2,600 after ten years.[7]

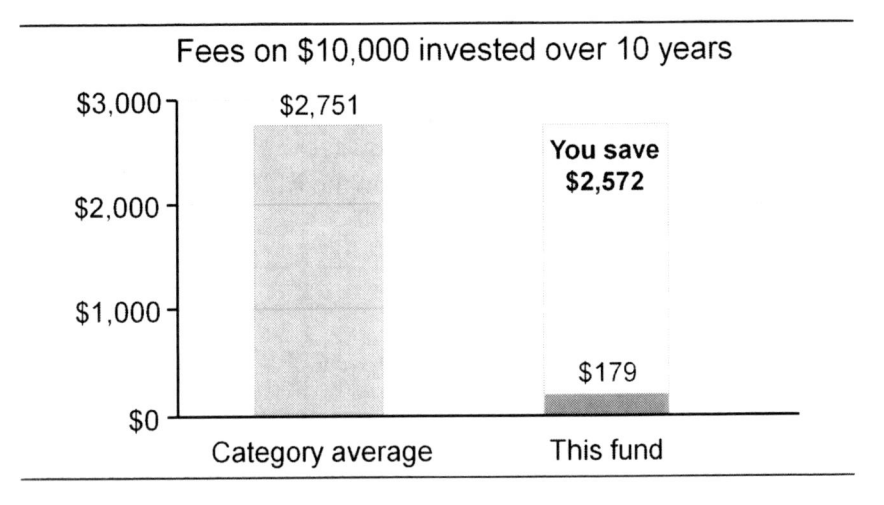

Fees on $10,000 invested over 10 years

Example: the index fund advantage

To understand the devastating impact of these costs, consider a 25-year old, Paul, who invests $100 per month in a Roth IRA until he is 65. In the next table, one column shows the amount he would earn using a historic stock market average captured with a low-cost index fund. The right column shows the amount Paul would earn with the same gross returns, but with a sales charge of 60 cents for each $100 investment and actively managed fund costs of 2% per year. At age

65 he would have earned $210,000 *less*, and that difference would continue to get worse.

Now if future returns are lower, then these costs take an even bigger bite out of what he would earn. Costs matter! Keep them low.[8]

EXAMPLE   Worker Invests $100/mo for 40 years

	Index Fund	Active Funds
Gross Returns	10%	10%
Expenses:		
Sales Charge	---	0.6%
Expense Ratio	0.07%	1.5%
Additional	0.01%	0.5%
Value at age 65	$ 519,691	$ 309,003

Unfortunately, some 401(k) plans do not offer any index funds at all. In that case, look for the largest, most diversified funds with the lowest fees.

Now, some of your savings will be in a taxable account where (guess what!) taxes are the third big cost that dramatically affects your return. We'll look at this in the next chapter.

Chapter Footnotes

Find this and other explanatory videos, smart tips, and links to useful resources at www.FinancingLife.org.

(1) "The stock market index fund was providing an annual return of 12.3 percent and the average equity fund was earning an annual return of 10.0 percent, the average fund investor was earning only 7.3 percent a year." *The Little Book of Common Sense Investing: The Only Way to Guarantee Your Fair Share of Stock Market Returns*, by John C. Bogle, 2007, p.51.

(2) *All About Index Funds*, by Richard A. Ferri, 2nd Edition, McGraw-Hill, 2007, p.25.

(3) *The Bogleheads' Guide to Investing*, by Larimore, Lindauer, and LeBoeuf, 2007, pp 110-116

(4) John C. Bogle, *The Little Book of Common Sense Investing: The Only Way to Guarantee Your Fair Share of Stock Market Returns*, 2007, p. 51.

(5) Ibid. , p.37.

(6) *In Investing, You Get What You Don't Pay For*, 2005 Keynote Speech by John C. Bogle, http://johncbogle.com/speeches/JCB_MS0205.pdf

(7) This is a screenshot from Vanguard Total Stock Market Index Fund Admiral Shares which had an expense ratio of 0.07% (subject to change). The minimum investment is $10,000, and the ticker symbol is VTSAX. This fund is also available in another class called Investor Shares with an expense ratio of 0.18%, a minimum investment of $3,000 and ticker symbol VTSMX.

(8) John C. Bogle, *The Little Book of Common Sense Investing: The Only Way to Guarantee Your Fair Share of Stock Market Returns*, 2007, p. 37.

Rule #8:

Minimize taxes

Two things every investor should know to be a smart taxpayer are that:

- Not all income is taxed the same, so

- You generally want to hold bonds in a retirement account and stocks in a taxable account.

To understand this, let's consider Sharon and Mark's retirement account. We always start with a long-term plan which includes choosing risk and asset allocation *before* worrying about taxes. They have decided that the correct risk level for their retirement portfolio is 60% stocks and 40% bonds, increasing the allocation to bonds by 1% every year.

Sharon and Mark (married, age 40)

Current Value	Risk Level (stocks / bonds)	Purpose
$120,000	60% / 40%	retirement
$ 38,000	*(very safe)*	buy house in 2-3 yrs
$ 5,000	*(very safe)*	emergency fund

Their preference is to own total stock market index funds, with 2/3 from US companies and 1/3 from international companies. For bonds, they chose a total US bond market index fund.

Desired Asset Allocation

Current Value	Risk Level (stocks / bonds)	Purpose
$120,000	60% / 40%	retirement

$48,000 Total US Stock Market Index Fund
$24,000 Total Foreign Stock Market Index Fund
$48,000 Total US Bond Market Index Fund

Later in this chapter we will learn how it is advantageous to hold these funds in different types of accounts. But first, we need to learn about the major types of accounts and their tax implications.

Taxable, tax-free, and tax-deferred accounts

You can have taxable, tax-free, and tax-deferred accounts. Tax-advantaged accounts are the most tax-efficient place to invest, so you'll want to take maximum advantage of these.

Sharon+Mark's Asset Locations

Taxable Accounts — Regular accounts

Tax-free Accounts — Roth IRA (*Individual Retirement Account*)

Tax-deferred Accounts — Traditional IRA, 401(k), *or* 403(b)

Sharon's been contributing to a Roth IRA with some of their after-tax earnings every year. Her contributions are with income that she has already paid taxes on. But the account's growth will never be taxed, so the ultimate earnings are much larger—a big advantage!

Mark has a 401(k) retirement program with his employer. This, like traditional IRA Accounts, is all tax-deferred. They pays no taxes on income he invests here, or on any growth of these investments, until he uses it during retirement when it all gets taxed as ordinary income. Best of all, his company matches some of his contributions.

Let's consider their tax situation. As they earn more income, the last dollars they earn get taxed at higher levels. Say they are in the 25% marginal tax bracket. While they pay less than 10% of their total gross income on federal income taxes, the important thing is that of the last dollar they earned in wages, 25% went to these taxes.

Example Tax Brackets (Actual rates change frequently)

Ordinary tax rates

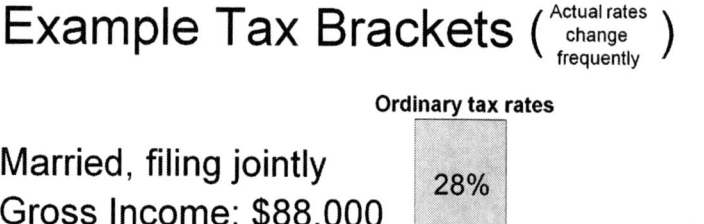

Married, filing jointly
Gross Income: $88,000
Federal Income Tax:
= $8,493
Effective tax rate: 9.7%
Marginal tax rate: 25%

28%
25%
15%
10%
0%

Now to the first point of this chapter: not all income is taxed the same.

Not all income is taxed the same

Let's consider how investments get taxed. It turns out that the interest and dividends that you earn from your bonds, bank CDs, and savings accounts are all taxed like ordinary income—or 25% for the investor in this example.

Now with stocks, you own a portion of these companies and they distribute some of their profits to you as dividends. Second, as the company grows, the value of the shares appreciate. So you hope to sell them for a higher price in the future. If you hold the stock for a long time and the price goes up, not only do you get to defer paying taxes on the appreciation until you sell it, but this long-term capital-gains tax is at a lower rate.

The next chart shows that there is a big difference in these tax rates! (Remember: actual rates change frequently. What you are learning here are the key concepts.)

There's more good news. Currently the earnings that are distributed every year as qualified dividends are also taxed at this lower rate!

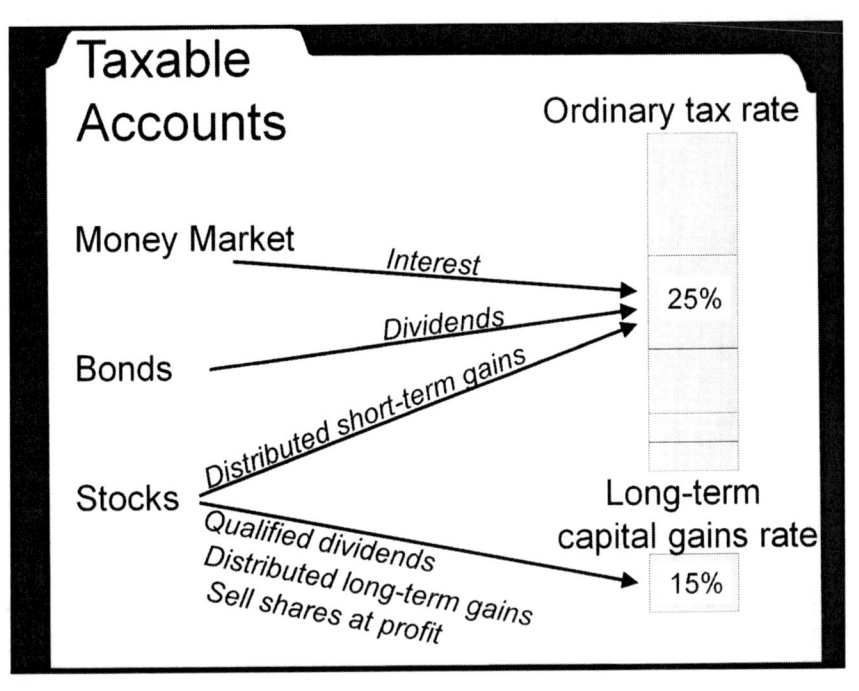

Now, some mutual funds that are actively managed do lots of buying and selling, trying to beat the market. This turnover creates extra capital gains that you have to declare and pay taxes on now, instead of deferring these into the future like you would prefer. The best mutual funds are going to have low-turnover in addition to being low-cost and widely diversified. *The best choices are usually index funds, but they aren't always. It's these attributes that are important.*

Desired Mutual Fund Attributes:

- ## Low turnover

- ## Low cost

- ## Widely diversified

Five steps to tax-efficient asset locations

We saw that not all income is taxed the same. The next chart ranks different kinds of mutual funds by tax efficiency. This is not sorting good funds from bad. Rather, it is to guide us to which account to hold each investment in. It makes a big difference.

Step 1: Determine Tax Efficiency

Most Tax Efficient

Tax-managed stock funds
Total US market stock index funds
Total international stock index funds

These are fine in **any** account.

Small-cap or mid-cap index funds
Value index funds
Low-yielding bonds or cash

Balanced funds (*bonds with stocks*)
Most bond funds
Active stock funds

Try to avoid these in a taxable account.

Real estate or REIT funds
High-turnover active funds
High-Yield Bonds

Least Tax Efficient

Getting back to our example: after they've considered risk and asset allocation, Sharon and Mark determine the tax efficiency of each of their investment assets. We want to place the bonds in their tax-deferred retirement account, or more precisely, those investments that

63

have the highest tax cost. This is the main point. So if you only remember one thing, remember this.

Sometimes the limited fund selection in a 401(k) does not include a good low-cost bond fund. If not, bonds can be allocated to a Roth account if there is "space"—meaning, it has grown large enough over time from regular contributions.

The next steps illustrate how to locate funds for tax efficiency by considering the three funds owned in this chapter's example.

Step 2: Place Least Efficient

Most Tax Efficient

Tax-managed stock funds
Total US market stock index fund
Total international stock index fund

Taxable Accounts

Small-cap or mid-cap index funds
Value index funds
Low-yielding bonds or cash

Tax-free Accounts

Balanced funds (bonds with stocks)   *alternative →*
Most bond funds
Active stock funds   *if good fund choices available*

Tax-deferred Accounts

Real estate or REIT funds
High-turnover active funds
High-Yield Bonds

Least Tax Efficient

Other recommendations: generally keep your foreign stocks in your taxable account where you can get a foreign tax credit.

Step 3: Place International Stock

Most Tax Efficient

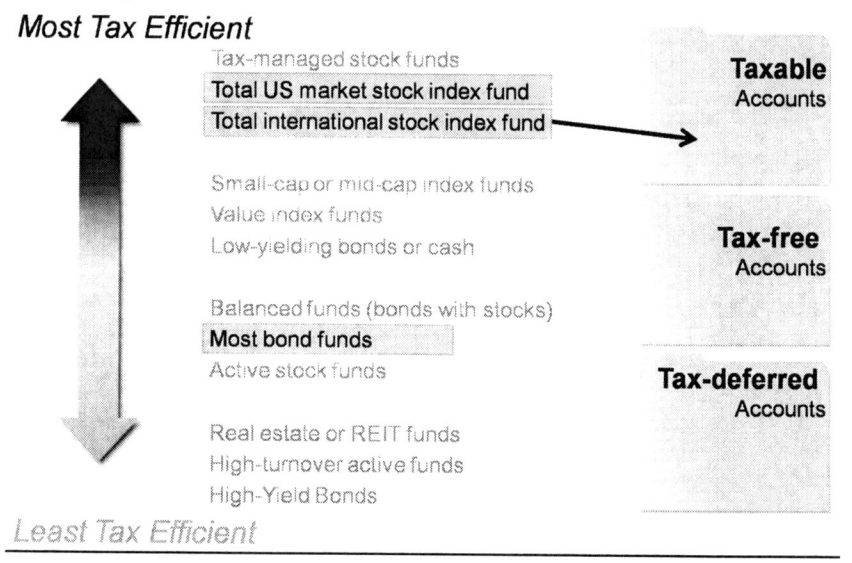

And usually put the fund with the highest expected return into a tax-free Roth IRA.

Step 4: High Growth to Roth

Most Tax Efficient

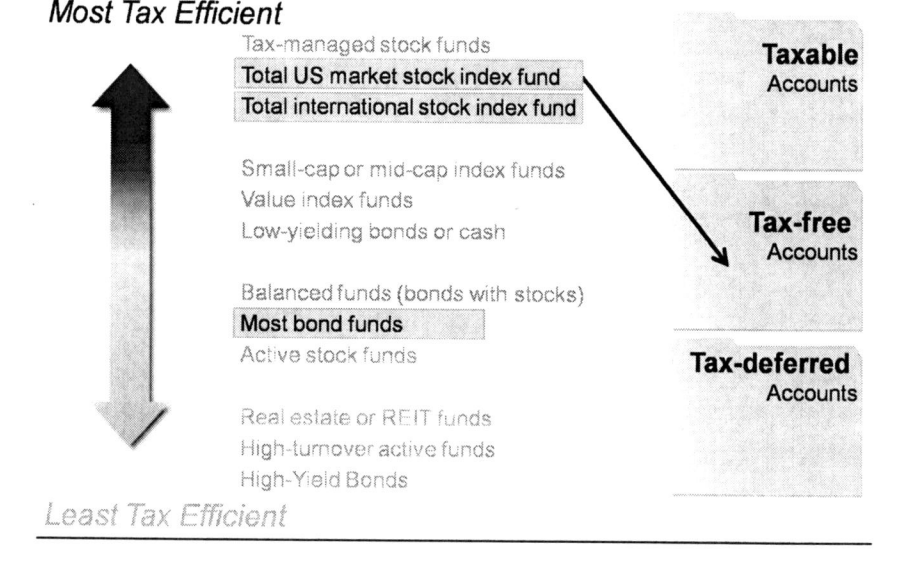

Fill up the remaining space in your tax-advantaged accounts with tax-efficient stock funds, and then hold the rest in a taxable account. For this example, here is how it ends up looking.

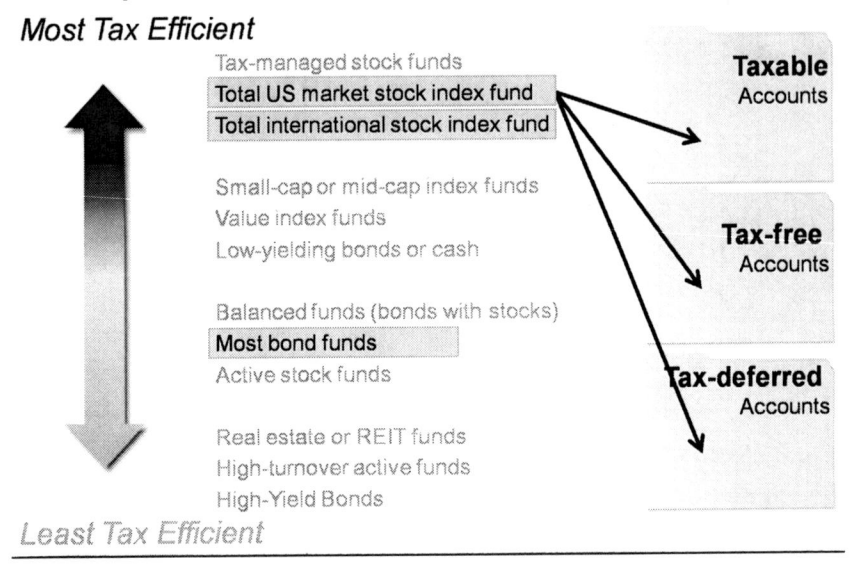

Step 5: Efficient Funds Anywhere

Most Tax Efficient

Tax-managed stock funds
Total US market stock index fund
Total international stock index fund

Taxable Accounts

Small-cap or mid-cap index funds
Value index funds
Low-yielding bonds or cash

Tax-free Accounts

Balanced funds (bonds with stocks)
Most bond funds
Active stock funds

Tax-deferred Accounts

Real estate or REIT funds
High-turnover active funds
High-Yield Bonds

Least Tax Efficient

There are many other benefits to having stock funds in a taxable account, so I'll provide you links to these topics if you want to explore them.

Advanced strategies

Tax Loss Harvesting:
www.bogleheads.org/wiki/Tax_Loss_Harvesting

Whether to Reinvest Dividends in a Taxable Account:
www.bogleheads.org/wiki/Whether_to_Reinvest_Dividends_in_a_Taxable_Account

Cost Basis Methods:
www.bogleheads.org/wiki/Cost_basis_methods

Specific Identification of Shares:
www.bogleheads.org/wiki/Specific_Identification_of_Shares

Placing Cash Needs in a Tax-Advantaged Account
www.bogleheads.org/wiki/Placing_Cash_Needs_in_a_Tax-Advantaged_Account

Chapter Footnotes

Find this and other explanatory videos, smart tips, and links to useful resources at www.FinancingLife.org.

This topic is discussed more completely in this wiki article: Principles of Tax-Efficient Fund Placement: http://www.bogleheads.org/wiki/Principles_of_Tax-Efficient_Fund_Placement

Another good discussion of this topic is in *The Only Guide to a Winning Investment Strategy You'll Ever Need*, by Larry Swedroe, 2005, pp 179-183.

Never underrate either the majesty of simplicity or its proven effectiveness as a long-term strategy for productive investing. Simplicity, indeed, is the master key to financial success.

—John C. Bogle, *Common Sense On Mutual Funds*

Rule #9:

Keep it simple

Hearing the truth about investing is empowering. Yes! You can do this! But it's imperative that you create a plan that you can stick to. Keeping it as simple as you can will help.

The magic that makes a plan work is to put something in writing. Something that you will look at and review every year. It forces you to write down what you are actually doing, and makes you realize what assumptions you are making.

Start wherever you are! Don't strive for perfection.

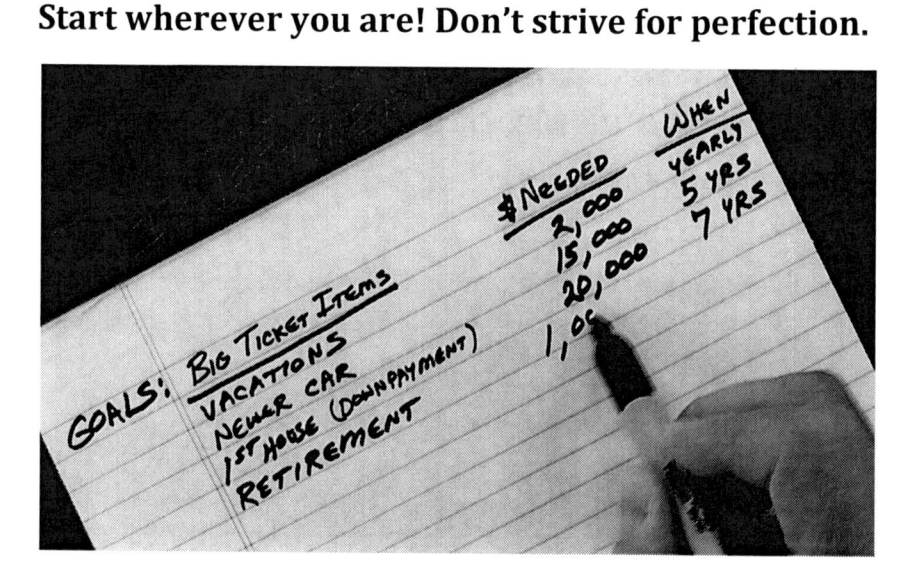

Write what you can about the big ticket items you can envision. You can always change these later. In a month, or a year, or two, or five, your goals will take shape and look something like this. Everybody's objectives are different. Most of us have near term goals that get dwarfed by what we'll eventually need for retirement. These are what motivate your most important habit: starting now and saving regularly. For instance: maybe you will decide to save by automatic paycheck investments; 5% of your gross income for short-term goals plus another 10% for retirement.

Your most important decision (stocks/bonds ratio)

Next is the most important decision—how much risk is appropriate for you to take on these investments. For your mid- to long-term goals, it's simply the ratio of stocks and bonds you own. It is essential that you own both. You need to be at a level that's appropriate for *you*.

The following chart is a little simplistic but it will remind you (1) that this is your most important decision, (2) the closer you are to needing money, the safer that amount should be invested, and (3) your long-term allocation must be managed to be very stable over time. Again, consider *ability, willingness, and need* to refine your plan.

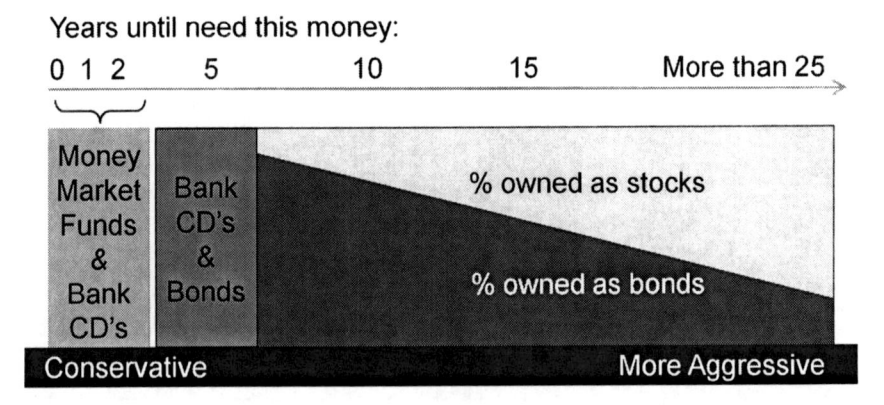

It is common for investors to gradually make their portfolios more conservative as they approach their retirement when they will rely on those savings. But not always. The following example is also an excellent plan. These investors (man and wife) have identified their appropriate level of risk, and the plan is both solid and simple.[1]

Example: Investment Policy Statement

This couple views all their investments together for both their short and long-term goals, and have decided to own a constant 60% stocks and 40% bonds every year until they purchase a home. Their stocks are further divided 3/4 US stocks and 1/4 foreign stocks. Any good-quality low-cost bond fund works fine. The type of bonds is far less important than the amount of bonds.

MY INVESTMENT PLAN

Goals:

Big Ticket Items	Money Needed	When
Newer car	$15,000 needed	in 5 Years
House (downpayment)	$20,000 needed	in 7 Years
Retirement	$1,000,000 needed	beginning in 25 Years

Saving:

10% gross income for retirement + 5% gross income for other.

Automatic paycheck investments.

Investment Philosophy:

"Buy-and-hold, long-term, all-market-index strategies, implemented at rock-bottom cost, are the surest of all routes to the accumulation of wealth." —John C. Bogle

71

Asset Allocation:

Maintain overall 60% stock + 40% bond allocation until home purchase to accommodate both short-term and long-term requirements. Assets diversified across major asset classes:

- U.S. stocks

- Foreign stocks (20-25% of all stock),

- Conventional bonds (high-quality, short to intermediate term)

Funds & Accounts:

- Use low cost mutual funds, preferably index funds, which do not overlap and provide maximum diversification across asset classes.

- Try to shelter tax-inefficient funds in tax-advantaged accounts.

Target Allocation:

VTSMX	*Total Stock Market Fund*	*45%*	**Taxable acct**
VGTSX	*Total Int'l Market Fund*	*15%*	**Roth IRA**
FIBIX	*Intermediate T-Bond Fund*	*40%*	**401k acct**
Money Market fund (covers 6 months of expenses)			**Taxable acct**

Other

- *Automate contributions wherever possible. Rebalance yearly.*

- *No market timing. Exact sub-allocations are not as important as maintaining the overall 60/40 stocks/bonds allocation.*

*** end of plan ***

You'll want to take maximum advantage of taxable and tax-advantaged accounts. These are for everybody.

When it comes to selecting specific funds, it is helpful to remind yourself what investment philosophy you believe in. This couple included this quote in their plan to help ground them in common sense. I liked it so this quote is in my own plan too.

> *"Buy-and-hold, long-term, all-market-index strategies, implemented at rock-bottom cost, are the surest of all routes to the accumulation of wealth."*
>
> —John C. Bogle

We talked a lot about what makes a good fund and which account you want to hold them in. This couple lists their fund selections and target allocations and adds these final comments: *"Automate future contributions wherever possible. Rebalance yearly. No market timing. Exact sub-allocations are not as important as maintaining the overall 60/40 stocks/bonds allocation."*

Every year they look at this Investment Plan and compare it with their actual investments. If stocks grew faster that year, they change their future automatic monthly investments to buy more bonds. Maintaining the 60/40 allocation keeps the risk at their desired level.

In years when the stock market plummets, rebalancing means buying more stocks. Appendix E shows an example. It is psychologically hard to rebalance in a drop, and you'll find a simple written *Investment Policy Statement* to be very helpful. You can do this if you have confidence that stocks will go up in the long run. Stocks are a long-term investment. There will be many bumps in the road: wars, recessions, high inflation, and stuff we haven't even thought of.

Find links to other plans in the footnotes below. You can do this! And most likely, you *must* invest wisely to accomplish your life dreams.

It doesn't need to be more complicated than this. Successful investing involves doing just a few things right, and avoiding serious mistakes.

Strive for a rough draft now

Just strive for a rough draft your first year, but make sure it is written. As you review it every year it will improve in a natural way as you continue to learn. Resist the temptation to gussy it up with needless bells and whistles. Pretty soon you'll have a robust plan and you'll be accomplishing your objectives—and financing your dreams. After all, that's why we do this, right?

Chapter Footnotes

Find this and other explanatory videos, smart tips, and links to useful resources at www.FinancingLife.org.

(1) While I favor plans that fit on one side of one sheet of paper, in practice they vary widely. You might find it constructive to look at some other plans here:
www.bogleheads.org/wiki/IPS#Real-World_IPS
and here:
www.bogleheads.org/forum/viewtopic.php?p=852539#852539

Rule #10:

Stay the course

Here's where it gets difficult for most of us—in fact, very difficult.

Tune out the noise

Intuitively, we understand the importance of sticking to our plan. Yet we're constantly receiving conflicting messages about how to be successful investors. For example, the mutual fund industry tells us that:

- Professionals have the best chance of picking stocks that will outperform, and

- A mutual fund that has outperformed the market in the past is likely to outperform the market in the future.

At the same time, the discount brokerage firms are telling us that:

- Picking stocks on your own is easy!

- You can time the market successfully with up-to-the-minute information.

Meanwhile, the mainstream financial media is bombarding us with a third group of messages, like:

- You can improve your performance by picking hot funds (particularly those mentioned in their show or magazine).

- If you watch the news enough and listen to enough economists/market analysts, you have a good chance of predicting the next market move.

So whom should we believe? Each of those sources seems like they should know what they're talking about.

The reality is that the primary goal of each of those parties is not to provide us with quality information, but rather to persuade us to consume their products (just like any other business). So we must tune them out and turn instead to unbiased sources of information (like academic studies). When we do, we encounter a few findings that have been confirmed time and again:

- Within each category of mutual funds, expenses are the best predictor of future performance.[1]

- Any investor—even a full-time professional—is unlikely to be able to reliably outperform the market.[2] And,

- Reliably predicting short-term market moves is impossible.[3]

And those facts lead us to this simple common-sense investment strategy.

The common sense strategy

1. Develop a workable plan.

2. Start saving now, not later. Time is your friend when you use the wondrous growth power of compound interest.

3. Own the appropriate amount of bonds. It is the ratio of stocks to bonds that controls your risk. This is far more important than which specific funds you choose.

4. Diversify, and hold on to your investments for as long as you possibly can before selling them.

5. Never try to time the market.

6. Use index funds when possible.

7. Keep all costs low, not just sales costs, but the recurring expense ratio, and hidden tax consequences.

8. Taxes are a very big cost that you can minimize, or defer.

9. Keep it simple.

10. And hardest of all: Stick To Your Plan!

"Stay the course" means that once you've chosen your portfolio, only sell to rebalance and maintain your risk level. Never sell based on greed or fear.

Imagine that you wake up tomorrow morning and the stock market is down 50% due to some huge global problem, like a nuclear war in the middle east, what will you do? If the answer is "sell" when it is down 50%, then you have too much in stocks. You are carrying more risk than you can live with.

A written plan helps immensely

A written Investment Policy Statement helps you rebalance in a market drop. Everyone is different. Not everyone can be cool in the line of fire. But knowing your limitations ahead of time and being able to admit them and select an appropriate level of risk and a plan that you can stick with is a wonderful pursuit of self knowledge.[4]

You can do this!

You can do this! Now when you get a question, and you will, you can turn to the Bogleheads wiki.

http://www.bogleheads.org/wiki/Main_Page

The Bogleheads have endearingly named themselves after John C. Bogle, the great champion of common sense investing. Join them online. You can find answers to common questions or books that are worth reading. And if you can't find your answer, you can always anonymously ask the Bogleheads discussion board—a group of friendly people that are amazingly generous with helpful feedback (to people with genuine questions).

Tune out the noise. Stick to these ten simple guidelines. Investing is just a small piece of fully living your life, but it's an important piece. It enables you to reach some of your most valued dreams.

Chapter Footnotes

Find this and other explanatory videos, smart tips, and links to useful resources at www.FinancingLife.org.

This chapter was highly inspired from chapter 12 (pp. 98-100) of *Investing Made Simple* by Mike Piper, and used with permission.

Also inspired by a well-worded posting by jidina80 on the bogleheads.org forum, and used with permission.

(1) See chapter about Rule#7: Keep costs low.

(2) See chapter about Rule #6: Use index funds when possible.

(3) See chapter about Rule#5: Never try to time the market.

Appendix A:
Simple rules vs. human nature

Why do people say "investing is *simple*, but not *easy?*" It's because we're humans. Successful investing is surprisingly simple, but plans are hard to stick with due to human nature. I'll illustrate how this is counterintuitive, but I can't do it better than the Bogleheads (the admirers of John C. Bogle, champion of common sense investing).

In times of crisis, a human instinct is:
"Don't just stand there! Do something!"
The Boglehead principle is:
"Don't do something. Just stand there."

Long-term investments need to be exactly that. Drama aside, Bogleheads don't just stand there. If the financial crisis is big enough to move an investor's stocks/bonds ratio out of their desired risk level, they might sell some bonds to buy more stocks. Rebalancing accomplishes a good thing: selling high and buying low, or sometimes selling low and buying lower. It is *not* market timing. It does not involve predicting. Read more about rebalancing in Appendix E. The key thing is to understand the basic concepts so that you have the confidence to *"stay the course."*

For most everything in our lives, the usual advice is:
"Stay informed!"
The Boglehead principle is:
"Ignore the noise."

Wisdom comes from lifelong learning. Bogleheads will be first to point you to good books. But don't mistake the chatter from the media, and others who are trying to sell you something, as being useful information.

The usual advice is:
"You get what you pay for."
The Boglehead principle is:
"We get to keep precisely what we don't pay for."

Remember this from Rule #6? It's key! But to accomplish it you may have to fend off some persuasive salesmen trying to convince you not to settle for settle for *average results* from index funds. Reread this book if you need to!

Unlike most things, investing is one where you set things up and then leave them alone. John C. Bogle commented that "successful investing involves just doing a couple of things right and avoiding any major mistakes."

Have you learned enough to do those few things right? Maybe. Or, are you still striving to find the perfect plan? Here's one more.

For many things we do in life:
"There is a single best answer."
But for investing, Bogleheads find this wisdom helpful:
"There are many roads to Dublin," and
"The greatest enemy of a good plan is the dream of a perfect plan."

Getting started with your first investment will help you learn. You can start with as little as $1,000, and some companies will waive this minimum requirement if you sign up for automatic contributions. Once you are invested, you'll find it much more interesting to read more and continue to learn. But this is where I'd like you to exercise some caution.

Many of the books at the bookstore are meant to appeal to our bad instincts and don't offer wise advice. As your learning progresses, you will be able to quickly distinguish the good books from the bad. Meanwhile, I suggest you start with books that are recommended either by me, the Bogleheads, or a trusted advisor. I point you to some good lists later in this book.

Appendix B:
Become a savvy buyer

A common belief is that there are smart professionals, with resources beyond our imagination, that are more capable of beating the average market return than we are.

I too know that there are excellent people actively managing mutual funds. But this short book has attempted to show that *after you pay their fees,* your probability of even achieving the average market return is low and gets worse with time.

Keep in mind that companies are *competing* for your investments and each company is trying to *sell* you their products and services. You need to be a savvy buyer. Remember, their marketing is excellent, so this can be hard to recognize.

Test yourself. Suppose this was their sales pitch. Can you see through this?

"We beat the S&P 500 index by 20% last year."

See the problem? This picture will give you a hint:

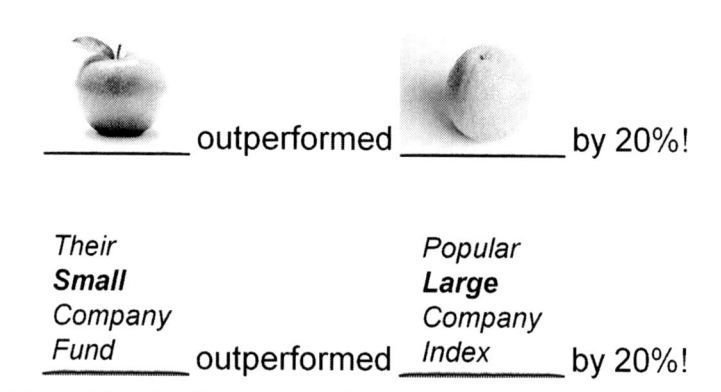

Beware the Marketing

_____ outperformed _____ by 20%!

| Their **Small** Company Fund | outperformed | Popular **Large** Company *Index* | by 20%! |

Yes! You get it. You can only compare apples with apples. You can't compare large company stocks with small company stocks any more than you can compare stocks with bond performance. They are different asset classes with different levels of risk. And when you recognize it from that perspective, you would know to find out more and compare it with the appropriate benchmark (e.g. an index fund of small company stocks for this example).

OK, test yourself again. This next one is going to be harder. Can you see through this?

"Our fund beat the S&P 500 index for the past five years."

Your first reactions are probably good ones—you ask to learn more about risk level and expenses. You are getting good! But keep going. A long track record is pretty compelling! Is this manager truly brilliant?

Simple random luck will make some people appear more brilliant than they really are. I'd like you to consider the following scenario. A thousand individuals are gathered together to participate in a contest. (Coin-Tossing Gurus?) A coin will be tossed and the contestants must guess whether it will come up heads or tails. Contestants who correctly guess the outcome of *five* consecutive tosses are declared winners and each receive the coveted title of "National Coin-tossing Guru of the Year."

Simple statistics tell us we can expect that after the first toss, five hundred participants will have guessed the outcome correctly. The other five hundred will have guessed incorrectly and thus are eliminated from the competition. After the second round, 250 participants will remain; and so on. *After five repetitions we would expect to have thirty remaining participants who would have guessed correctly all five times and earned their guru status!* What probability would you attach to the likelihood that those thirty gurus would win the next coin-toss competition? (Hint: 50%—the same as for you!) I chose a coin-toss example, because we humans tend to give too much weight to recent experience—perhaps like the mutual funds ranked with five stars?

Now how do you feel about the active fund manager that beat the market average five years in a row? Was it superior intelligence? Keep in mind that there are *thousands* of mutual funds.

Or, are we fooled by randomness? Since funds are competing for your investment dollars, I want you to have healthy skepticism about their sales pitches.

Remember, the stock market *average* return is exactly that. If there were no costs involved, the winners that over-performed would exactly equal the losers that under-performed. Because, together they comprise the whole market and earn the "total market return".

Well, *with no costs*—50/50—that sounds pretty similar to the odds in our coin-tossing example doesn't it?

The grim reality is that the odds of beating the market average *after* mutual fund expenses is much worse. That's why the argument for considering index funds is so compelling

"Costs matter!" John Bogle constantly shows us. *"You get to keep what you don't give away."*

John Bogle writes in his *Little Book of Common Sense Investing*, "Once you recognize this fact, you can see that the index fund is guaranteed to win not only over time, but every year, and every month and week, even every minute of the day. Because no matter how long or short the time frame, the gross return in the stock market, minus intermediation costs, equals the net return earned by investors."

If you are *still* tempted to choose what looks like a manager with superior intelligence with fees and other costs that are lower than your expected return premium, then consider the market effect of new money attracted into that fund, and the manager needing to repeat that genius the next year by investing 10 to 100 times last year's amount. Those opportunities are quite different!

*Spend less time studying your investments
and more time studying yourself.*

—Jason Zweig, in *Money*, Nov 1998

Appendix C:
Example startup portfolios

Everybody must start somewhere. Your first investment can simply be one fund. If you are starting with $1,000, consider a "target retirement fund." Ignore the name. This is just a perfect fund to save for anything—house, kid's college, or retirement. While there are many of these with various retirement dates in their names, do not pay attention to the dates either. Instead, choose the one with the stock/bond ratio you seek. For instance, if you conclude that owning 67% stocks and 33% bonds is right for you, then consider this fund:

> Vanguard Target Retirement 2020 Fund (VTWNX)
> (stocks/bonds = 67%/33%) (expense ratio = 0.16%)

That's a terrific expense ratio! And this type of balanced funds is gets more conservative every year (so the stocks/bonds ratio I print here is always out-of-date). I don't care where you invest, but Vanguard's target retirement funds can be used as a benchmark as you compare alternatives.

As soon as you have grown this to $20,000 you can exchange this for some individual funds with still lower combined expenses (see next page). With only these three funds, investors can create a low cost, broadly diversified portfolio that is very easy to manage and rebalance. This can also be more tax efficient if you locate these funds in accounts as described earlier.

Fidelity also has an outstanding family of funds, called Spartan Funds, so I'll include an example using these as well on the next page. Remember, all these examples approximate a 67/33 risk level which might not be appropriate for you. You must decide this.

Find more simple portfolio ideas at the Bogleheads wiki:
http://www.bogleheads.org/wiki/Lazy_Portfolios

Vanguard: The combined expense ratio for this portfolio = 0.19%.

% Allocation	Fund	Fund Symbol	Notes, and expense ratio
33%	Vanguard Total Bond Market Index Fund	VBMFX	$3,000 minimum ER = 0.20%
47%	Vanguard Total Stock Market Index Fund	VTSMX	$3,000 minimum ER = 0.17%
20%	Vanguard Total International Stock Index Fund	VGTSX	$3,000 minimum ER = 0.22%

Check their website for the most current information.

Fidelity: The combined expense ratio for this portfolio = 0.15%.

% Allocation	Fund	Fund Symbol	Notes, and expense ratio
33%	Fidelity Spartan Intermediate Treasury Bond Index Fund	FIBIX	$2,500 minimum ER = 0.20%
47%	Fidelity Spartan Total Market Index Fund	FSTMX	$2,500 minimum ER = 0.10%
20%	Fidelity Spartan International Index Fund	FSIIX	$2,500 minimum ER = 0.20%

Check their website for the most current information.

Appendix D:
Dollar cost averaging

We often don't miss money that we never see. And we often make regrettable mistakes when we let timing sneak into purchase decisions. So setting up automatic investment contributions has become a time-proven path to success. By investing equal amounts regularly (such as $300 monthly) in a particular investment, more shares are purchased when prices are low and fewer shares are purchased when prices are high. The point of this is to lower the average cost per share of the investment, giving the investor a lower overall cost for the shares purchased over time.

Example #1: payroll-timed contributions of $300 for six months.

Month	Amount	Price	Shares
1	$ 300	$ 5	60
2	$ 300	$ 6	50
3	$ 300	$ 5	60
4	$ 300	$10	30
5	$ 300	$12	25
6	$ 300	$10	30
Total	$1,800	$7.05	255

The average market price for this example is $8.00.
(5+6+5+10+12+10)/6=$8.00)

Your average cost per share is $1,800/255 = approximately $7.05.

The point is that this both removes the temptation of spending (by automatically investing) and takes the emotion out of investing. You don't have to guess when to purchase shares to get a better price (because you can't do that).

Compare this with a different situation—that of holding that $1,800 back at the first month with the intention of investing.

Example #2: You wish to invest a lump sum of money.

Maybe you inherit a lump sum of money. You have it in a money market account and you wish to invest it into a security that is expected to trend up over time. For this situation, stretching out that investment over a year or two using dollar cost averaging would not be a sound investment strategy. Lump sum investing will always produce a higher *expected return*, because it immediately moves your funds from an asset class with lower expected returns to one with a higher expected return. But remember, *expected returns* are not a guarantee. If your goal of minimizing your potential regret is actually greater than achieving the highest expected return, consider dollar cost averaging over a short period, perhaps a 4 to 6 months, to reduce the chance of buying just before a crash. Then as the market fluctuates, you buy more when it is low and less when it is high.

Appendix E: Rebalancing

Investing is a long-term proposition so it is pointless to watch the daily flutter of the stock market. But, an annual checkup makes sense. This is all about maintaining your appropriate level of risk.

If you did careful introspection and decided that 60% / 40% was the appropriate ratio of stocks and bonds for you yesterday, then you should seriously question yourself if you are tempted to change that if the stock market has a dramatic day tomorrow. Yes, change it when your personal situation changes in a significant and unexpected way. But don't do this lightly—you run the great risk of introducing your emotions into your investing decisions.

View rebalancing as a legitimate way to execute a "buy low" and "sell high" strategy—compared to emotion-based timing decisions. This works for any two funds. But to illustrate, consider a portfolio with a stock fund and a bond fund. Your desired allocation is 60% stocks, 40% bonds. You originally bought $6,000 stocks in Fund A, and $4,000 bonds in Fund B.

Scenario 1: stocks fall $1,100 and bonds grow $100. Now the stocks are only about 54% ($4,900/$9,000) of the portfolio—significantly off plan. So investor sells $500 of the bond fund to buy $500 more of the stock fund. The rebalanced portfolio is now $5,400 stocks and $3,600 bonds, back to 60% / 40%.

Scenario 2: both have a good year. The stock fund grows $1900 and the bond fund grows $100. Now the stocks are nearly 66% ($7,900/$12,000) of the portfolio—clearly a riskier portfolio because of the higher percentage in stocks. So investor sells $700 of the stock fund to buy $700 more of the bond fund. The rebalanced portfolio is $7,200 stocks and $4,800 bonds, back to 60% / 40%.

In all cases, rebalancing keeps the risk in an investor's portfolio at the desired level and the investor sells the asset that has done well to buy the asset that has done poorly.

You can keep it simple and do this annually. This works out nicely if your plan calls for holding gradually more bonds every year since that takes a little monitoring.

Some investors also choose to rebalance when the stocks in their portfolio differ from their target allocation by +/-5%. So using the above example with a target of 60% stocks and 40% bonds, the investor would rebalance anytime the stock portion grows to be above 65% of the portfolio, or falls below 55%.

Another strategy is to steer new contributions towards the asset whose level is lower than the target. For example, a couple invests $100 in new money after every paycheck with an automatic investment in their bond fund. After a significant decline in the stock market they change this to automatically purchase their stock funds instead.

These strategies (1) provide bonus returns from "selling winners" to "buy losers," (2) provide methods that remove emotions from the buy/sell decisions, and (3) maintain an investor's desired level of risk.

This is not market timing! There is no guessing about the future here. This is a strategy built around maintaining your desired level of risk so that you both achieve your goals and sleep well at night.

Some investors find it daunting to sell bonds to buy stocks right after a big drop in the stock market. If you are among those who would have difficulty doing this, you may want to consider "target retirement funds", which automatically rebalance as necessary to maintain a consistent asset allocation.

Appendix F:
Low-cost mutual fund providers

Be clear about this:

- You don't need lots of mutual funds to be diversified. Even one can do just fine.
- You don't need to use lots of mutual fund providers. That's a total misreading of what it means to be diversified! Keep it simple.

Rick Ferri's book, *All About Asset Allocation*, lists 26 mutual fund companies that have at least some funds with fees less than 0.50 percent and no sales load. So it is very likely that you have some good choices if you are already invested with one of these. I choose to offer just these three points about this topic.

Simplify. The fewer companies that you invest with, the simpler your life becomes when you need choose funds, do your income taxes, rebalance, or transfer money. So, when possible, consolidate with the company that works best for you.

The Vanguard Group is the investment management company founded by John C. Bogle. Mr. Bogle is credited with the creation of the first index fund available to individual investors, the popularization of index funds generally, and driving costs down across the mutual fund industry. The company is owned by the mutual funds which are owned by the investors, so we are bound with common interests. Find them at **www.vanguard.com**.

Fidelity Investments is one of the largest mutual fund and financial services groups in the world, so it is very likely that they might manage your retirement program. Their low-cost family of funds all have "Spartan" in their names, and this set is sufficient to meet most needs. I also particularly like their web site which allows me to sell individual lots of stocks in my taxable account. Find them at **www.fidelity.com**.

"Invest your time actively and your money passively."

—Michael LeBoeuf, Ph.D., author

Free high-definition streaming videos

Our goal is to help put the "common" back in *common sense investing*. One of the fun ways to reach out to a new and broader audience is by making short instructional videos available online.

Printed and ebooks provide readers the ability to quickly scan and pick out topics of interest, study interesting charts at a leisurely pace, or reference key points later. The bite-size videos provide an opportunity to bring these dry subjects to life and illustrate complicated topics in a more compelling way.

Here's a link to our YouTube channel:
http://www.youtube.com/user/FinancingLife101

Our website at www.FinancingLife.org embeds Vimeo videos.
Here are some viewing tips:

Share with your friends.

Expand to full screen.
Use ESC key to return.

Volume

Tip: If you pause, the video will continue to load your buffer so it will play smoothly when you resume.

Tip: Resolution will adjust to bandwidth available. Choose HD, or 720p, for best picture if you have high bandwidth.

Watch all ten rules in high-definition streaming video. Share with friends!

Please share these videos with your friends! They are free!

The Financing Life collection includes short online videos (free) and books that follow a small number of simple investment principles that have been shown over time to produce the best results. These ideas come from the investing philosophy of Vanguard-founder Jack Bogle. Some of these ideas are distilled from Nobel prize-winning financial economics research on topics like Modern Portfolio Theory and Capital Asset Pricing Model. But they are really very easy to understand and to implement, and they work. In fact, the basis of all of these principles is the idea that successful investing is not a complicated process, and can be accomplished by anyone with a small amount of effort.

Find future books and free online videos at www.financinglife.org.

Books I recommend

The chapter footnotes include some good ideas for further reading, but there are a lot of other terrific books and websites. Be careful—the majority of stuff is either trying to sell you something, or is about speculating in stocks and bonds (think gambling) rather than investing. I keep my recommendations up-to-date online here:

www.financinglife.org/investing-books/

The Bogleheads group have similar lists—all worthy of your consideration:

www.bogleheads.org/readbooks.htm and

bogleheads.org/wiki/Books:_Recommendations_and_Reviews

Your goal should be to become a knowledgeable investor. With that, most people can manage their own investments and be smart about hiring specialized help when needed. Few need advanced expertise. My website attempts to help you discover the lesson you may want to learn next. For instance, most of my readers are advanced-beginners and might consider phrases—like these—for links to suggestions about what to learn next, book suggestions and web resources.

- "I try to pick a few winners—like Warren Buffett does."
- "To me, 'speculating' and 'investing' seem like the same thing."
- "I watch the news and read the money magazines to choose the best funds."
- "I choose only no-load five star funds, so I know I own the best funds at the lowest cost."
- "I don't think frugal is a four letter word."

You can find this article with links to suggested books and websites at this web page address:

www.financinglife.org/book-recommendations/guidance

Acknowledgments

Common sense investing is an idea worth spreading. I think it is life-changing when people realize that they can take control of their finances, and that it is revealed as *common sense* when presented properly (as John Bogle does so eloquently).

I am tremendously indebted to all who participate at the Bogleheads.org. What a collection of generous, knowledgeable, and polite individuals! I have learned from respected authors and other experts, and sharpened my understanding with the give-and-take between the forum participants. It's incredible, and even behind the scenes people are contributing, moderating, and administering this organization as a public service. I'm so proud to be a part of it in even my modest little way.

A big thank you to Larry Swedroe for reviewing the book and providing valuable feedback.

A special tip-of-the-hat to award-winning author Jeff Lehman who reviewed several versions of this book and gave valuable feedback.

Thank you to friends and family, who helped me find this way of giving back.

Finally, I reserve my greatest appreciation for my wonderful wife, Jennifer, for all her love, encouragement, and support.

About the author

Rick Van Ness is a successful private investor and retired executive who provides investor education through online videos, short books, and workshops. Rick has an engineering degree from Cornell University and a MBA in Finance from New York University. His background in engineering and business provides him with the excellent basis for understanding and teaching investments and financial planning.

Rick provides unbiased education. He helps students understand the teachings of the most widely respected economists and financial planners. Students learn that investing smart is simple (not easy) and to take charge of their own finances on their paths to achieving rich and fulfilling lives. He is President of GrowthConnection LLC.

Neither Rick Van Ness nor GrowthConnection LLC sell any investment products or services, and do not provide individual investment advice. He educates you without self-interest (other than the joy he always gets from hearing from readers).

Connect with me online!

Website: **www.FinancingLife.org**
Email: rick@financinglife.org

Workspace: Start your plan

Print a copy of this workspace at: **www.FinancingLife.org/worksheets/**

<u>Emergency Funds:</u> You should have enough money, readily available, to cover 3-6 months of expenses for your most basic living needs. Stuff happens. This is to cover you until you are back on your feet. Where is your cash reserve?

Name of account:_____

Tip: Bank fees are expensive and unnecessary. If you accidently overdraw you bank account do two things: (1) call the bank and ask for a one-time waiver (you need to ask for this), and (2) consider keeping a minimum balance of $1000 to prevent this.

<u>Debt:</u> Some debt (e.g. school loans, home mortgage) can be part of good investing. But not always—home values plunged during the past decade, putting many homeowners "underwater". Stay aware of the interest rate you are paying on each loan. Sometimes your best investment strategy begins by paying off these loans.

Credit card debt is "like having TNT in your basement". Only use them if you can make every single payment *in-full* and *on-time*!

<u>Loans</u>	<u>Balance Due</u>	<u>Interest rate</u>
_____	_____	_____
_____	_____	_____
_____	_____	_____
_____	_____	_____

<u>Tax Rate:</u> To be a tax-savvy investor you must become aware of the tax bracket you are in. As you saw in Rule #8, this is not your total taxes divided by your total income, but rather it is a much higher number—the percentage of the next dollar you earn that will go to taxes. It is also called your "marginal tax bracket."
What is yours?

_____ % = Federal income tax

_____ % = State of residence income tax rate

<u>Goals:</u> start a list of dreams, and ballpark how much money they will need.

Big Ticket Items	Money Needed?	When?
_____	_____	_____
_____	_____	_____
_____	_____	_____
_____	_____	_____
_____	_____	_____
_____	_____	_____
_____	_____	_____
_____	_____	_____

Retirement: was retirement among your dreams? For most people this is going to require more savings than all other goals. This exercise will get you started. Every year that you reconsider this number you can make it more accurate. *Don't leave this blank.*

Ballpark income required: $ _____ / year
If you don't have any idea,
consider your parents, or use
75% of your current income.

Less social security benefit: less $ _____ / year
Tip: check the statement the
Social Security Administration
mails to you every year.

Less pension benefits: less $ _____ / year
(many jobs don't have this)

Equals retirement needs
to be financed by savings: = $ _____ / year

Multiply by 25 to get the
size of portfolio that you   x 25
might safely draw from at
4% per year for 30 years.
This includes cost-of-living
and inflation: = $ _____

Savings Plan:

Where should you put your first investment? Here is the general rule of thumb for investing priority towards your *long-term* goals:

1. 401(k)/403(b) up to the company match. This is first because the company match is free money. If your company does this, this is like giving yourself a raise.

2. Max out Roth. For most young people this is the next best place because of flexibility and unconstrained fund selection.

3. Max out 401(k)/403(b). This provides a way to shelter larger amounts of current income for retirement. But these programs offer limited fund selection; they are not all excellent. If you change employers, consider rolling this over to a traditional IRA with a firm that offers superb low-cost index funds.

4. Taxable Investing. Use taxable accounts for investments you anticipate using when you are younger. This is listed fourth to encourage you to first take full advantage of retirement accounts for money you won't need until you are age 60.

Saving regularly needs to be your most important habit. How will you get started? How can you put this on auto-pilot (automatic payroll investments)? What commitments will you make to yourself?

New annual contributions to YOUR taxable account:

_____

_____

New annual contributions to YOUR tax-advantaged accounts:

_____

_____

New annual contributions to SPOUSE's tax advantaged accounts:

_____

_____

How Much Risk is Appropriate for You?

Your *ability to take risk* is determined by your investment horizon and the stability of your income. How do you rate yourself?

Is your emergency cash reserve adequate? _____

Are you in a profession with high career stability? _____

Does your net worth exceed your needs? _____

Are you young with a long investment horizon? _____

Your *willingness to take risk* relates to your ability to withstand the ups and downs of the market without getting nervous and making changes to your asset allocation. Selling in the face of a decline is about the worst thing you can do. Here is a table offered by author Larry Swedroe, based on history, showing the amount of decline for various stock/bond allocations:

Percentage Stocks in your portfolio	Potential Loss in a Bad Year
20%	5%
30%	10%
40%	15%
50%	20%
60%	25%
70%	30%
80%	35%
90%	40%
100%	50%

Some argue that most investors should not own less than 20%, nor more than 80%, in stocks—primarily to enjoy the benefit described in Rule #4 and known as the Modern Portfolio Theory advantage. But, you know yourself best. How much exposure to stocks:

a) Would make you uncomfortable?_____

b) Are you willing to take?_____

Finally, your *need to take risk* is determined by your saving plan and the rate of return required to meet your financial goals. At your rate of saving, is the market return for an appropriate mix of stocks and bonds likely to meet your goals?

_____

_____

_____

~ ~ ~

There are other ways to determine an asset allocation, including several rules of thumb:

- Your age in bonds. So, if you are 40 years old, then use a 60/40 (stocks/bonds) asset allocation.

- 110 minus your age = percentage of portfolio in stocks (110-40 yrs old = 70/30 asset allocation)

- 120 minus your age = percentage of portfolio in stocks (120-40 yrs old = 80/20 asset allocation)

~ ~ ~

In Rule #3 we addressed asset allocation, specifically the ratio of stocks/bonds, as *your most important investment decision.* This decision is all about finding the right level of risk for you, and having a plan that matches your needs. As you think about your ability, willingness, and need to take risk you can see that this is multi-dimensional. It's hard. Some investors find questionnaire's like this to be helpful:

https://personal.vanguard.com/us/FundsInvQuestionnaire

Your Desired Asset Allocation:

1. Stocks/bonds allocation: (e.g. 80/20) _____

2. International allocation for stocks: usually this is a percentage of the total stocks value, instead of a percentage of the entire portfolio value, and commonly ranges from 20-50% of total stock value.

Pro: Higher percentage allocation better matches the world market.

Con: International stocks have more expensive cost of ownership.

Tip: The percentage you choose is much less important than sticking to your decision.

How much of your stocks will be foreign? _____

3. Do you have other subcategory breakdowns that are important to you? _____

_____

_____

_____

_____

Current Investments: view your long-term investments as a whole. Combine all accounts held by yourself and your spouse. (Most people do not include their house since they'll need to live somewhere.)

Taxable Accounts (combine both You and Spouse)
(Include cash for investing. Do not include emergency funds.)

% of Total	Investment Name	Ticker Symbol	Expense Ratio
10 %	Total Stock Market Index	(ABCDE)	0.20%
10 %	Int-term Treasury Bonds	(ABCDE)	0.20%
_____	_____	_____	____
_____	_____	_____	____
_____	_____	_____	____

Your Roth (tax-free account)

% of Total	Investment Name	Ticker Symbol	Expense Ratio
8 %	Total Stock Market Index	(ABCDE)	0.20%
_____	_____	_____	____
_____	_____	_____	____

Your IRA, 401(k), 403(b) (tax-deferred accounts)

% of Total	Investment Name	Ticker Symbol	Expense Ratio
12 %	Total Stock Market Index	(ABCDE)	0.20%
20 %	Int-term Treasury Bonds	(ABCDE)	0.20%
_____	_____	_____	____

_____ _____ _____ _____

_____ _____ _____ _____

Spouse's Roth

% of Total	Investment Name	Ticker Symbol	Expense Ratio
20 %	*Total Stock Market Index*	*(ABCDE)*	*0.20%*

_____ _____ _____ _____

_____ _____ _____ _____

Spouse's IRA, 401k, 403b

% of Total	Investment Name	Ticker Symbol	Expense Ratio
20 %	*Total Stock Market Index*	*(ABCDE)*	*0.20%*

_____ _____ _____ _____

_____ _____ _____ _____

_____ _____ _____ _____

_____

100% Important Note: *Total of all accounts together (not each account individually) adds up to 100%.*

Notes:

Notes:

Index

Did you find <u>at least</u> <u>one</u> good idea from this short book? If so, please consider writing a quick and honest review on my website or wherever you bought it. Your review will encourage others to take charge of their finances and achieve their dreams!

Thanks!
Rick

CPSIA information can be obtained at www.ICGtesting.com
Printed in the USA
LVOW05s0842010414

379680LV00032BC/1715/P

9 780985 800413